6⁸⁵

NOTABLE
ILLINOIS
WOMEN

Illustration copyright © 1976
by Michael J. Payne

printed by
Desaulniers Printing Company
Milan, Illinois

ISBN 0-940286-52-1

Illustration Credits

By Michael J. Payne:
Jane Addams
Mary Ann Bickerdyke
Mahalia Jackson
Mary Harris Jones
Harriet Monroe
Bertha Palmer
Myrtle Walgreen
Frances Willard

By David R. Collins:
Marguerite Brooks
Lorraine Hansberry
Archange Ouilmette
Lucy Perkins

NOTABLE ILLINOIS WOMEN

by
David R. Collins
and
Evelyn Witter

Illustrations by:
Michael J. Payne and David R. Collins

QUEST PUBLISHING
Rock Island, Illinois

DEDICATION

Wife, mother, friend, leader — in her lifetime Edythe Greenway was all of these, meeting each task with devotion, spirit, kindness and compassion. This book is respectfully dedicated to the memory of this extraordinary woman.

CONTENTS

INTRODUCTION

What is Illinois?

Geographers might answer, "It's a midwestern state, extending 385 miles from north to south and 270 miles across."

Geologists might reply, "It's flat, rolling plains which has a wealth of mineral resources, especially oil, coal and limestone."

Historians might emphasize, "It's a state that became the twenty-first to join the Union on December 3, 1818."

Of course, all the above answers are correct. But Illinois is more than a location, soil and a historical date. Illinois is people — people with hopes and dreams of building a better life for themselves and those around them. Illinois is men, women, boys and girls seeking to be useful and to find enjoyment in living.

Millions of people have played roles in the past history of Illinois. Each person has been a vital individual to family, friends and community. But in some cases, that individual community transcends all boundaries of place and time. The efforts of Frances Willard as President of the Women's National Christian Temperance Union in 1882 directly affects the efforts of current members of the organization. Each issue of Poetry Magazine published today is a tribute to the work of Harriet Monroe seventy-five years ago. Hull House, the settlement home opened by Jane Addams at the turn of the century, still serves as a model for others across the world.

Yes, women of Illinois have contributed to the quality of life in many ways. Some have independently trailblazed, while others have shared daring new paths with their husbands. It is these stories that offer hope and inspiration to others.

This volume of NOTABLE WOMEN OF ILLINOIS is an extention of ILLINOIS WOMEN – BORN TO SERVE, originally commissioned and printed by the Illinois Women's Clubs as a bicentennial project in 1976. The original effort has been expanded and updated. NOTABLE WOMEN OF ILLINOIS represents an appropriate spotlight to the strength and courage, the creativity and talent, the energy and enthusiasm that these individuals displayed.

David R. Collins
Moline, Illinois

Evelyn Witter
Milan, Illinois

ILLINOIS

The Northwest Territory was organized in 1787. American authority did not become effective in Illinois until about 1790. About this time a few American settlers began to move into the region.

Settlement was seriously impeded by the Indian troubles which accompanied the War of 1812.

At the end of the War, settlers came with a rush so that in 1818 the territory had the 40,000 population required for admission to the Union.

Illinois was admitted to the Union on December 3, 1818.

Kaskaskia was the first state capital, but in 1820 the state offices were moved to Vandalia. Twenty years later the capital was moved again. This time, Springfield, was made the state capital.

During all the time when Illinois was becoming a state, pioneer women and Indian women were learning that they had to know and understand each other if they were to live their lives together on the great prairie.

The following story is about an Indian woman and a white woman. It is a reflection and example of the bravery, intelligence, and compassion that frontier women displayed in the development of the great state of Illinois.

SQUAW BREAD

A lively spring morning brightened the Illinois prairie near Rock River. Theodosia Steeb, tall and sturdy for her 16 years, was busy kneading bread dough on the rough-hewn worktable. Suddenly she got the feeling she was being watched.

Turning, she saw standing in the open doorway an Indian squaw with a sleeping papoose on her back.

The squaw was not much older than Theodosia. Her smooth skin, drawn tightly over high cheekbones, gave her face a meager look.

"Wh-what do you want?" Theodosia managed to stammer as she tightly gripped the table.

The squaw kept silent and searched noiselessly about the cabin, stopping once to listen for sounds.

"I-I'm alone," Theodosia gasped.

The squaw seemed to understand though she did not answer. Quickly she glanced at the bubbling caldron, then at the amount of dough, then at the hunting knives in their rack near the fireplace.

Suddenly she sprang to the rack, then grasping a knife, approached Theodosia.

"Oh-please-" begged Theodosia.

Knife in hand the Indian woman moved stealthily forward until she reached the table. With a deft stroke she cut off a piece of dough and dropped it into the rendering pot.

Before Theodosia could retrieve her thoughts, the squaw was fishing the dough out of the kettle with the fireside ladle. While it was still sizzling she devoured the dough.

Again and again the squaw cut off chunks of dough, threw them into the caldron and hungrily stuffed them into her mouth.

Finally she reached out to touch Theodosia's hand. It was a gentle touch, a touch which transmitted gratefulness and apology, and a plea for forgiveness.

Theodosia's sympathetic response was immediate. "I know, you were hungry," she said. "I'm glad you came!"

A smile of friendship brightened both faces as the white girl and the Indian squaw looked deeply into each other's eyes. At that moment, in the log cabin on the Illinois prairie, there was a bond of understanding between two people of different races that was more genuine than any of the pacts which had been drawn up between their two peoples.

Soon the Indian woman moved toward the door and out again into the open prairie.

After that, whenever Theodosia made bread, she cut off a piece of unrisen dough and fried it in boiling fat. She called it Squaw Bread.

For generations now my family has made that same kind of bread. Today, whenever I make rolls, I fry Squaw Bread for my little girl. And as she eats, she always asks me to tell her the story about her great-great-grandmother and the Indian Squaw.

Evelyn Witter

Notable
Illinois
Women

JANE ADDAMS
1860 - 1935

Silently the small girl slipped out the door of the Sunday School classroom. She looked up and down the hallway. There was no one in sight.

Down the hall and up the stairs the girl ran. Moments later she pushed open the front door of the church and started down the steps.

"Jennie! Jennie Addams! Where are you going in such a hurry?"

Slowly the girl turned around to look up at her father. The tall, well-dressed man towered about his six-year-old daughter.

"But Papa, you mustn't be seen here talking to me," Jane said. She looked around nervously, afraid other people might be close by. "People will think less of you."

Mr. Addams shook his head. "What a foolish notion, Jennie. Where did you get such a silly thought? I shall be very happy to be seen anywhere, at any time with you."

Resting a loving hand on his daughter's shoulder, John Addams escorted young Jane down the steps and along the streets of Cedarville. Happily he stopped to introduce his daughter to people they met.

The admiration and love Jane Addams felt toward her father brought her joy and suffering. Born September 6, 1860, Laura Jane Addams was sickly and frail. With her mother's death when Jane was only two, she quickly turned to her father for attention. In the big family home, young Jane followed her father everywhere.

But in public, Jane wanted no one to know they were related. She saw her father as handsome, dignified, a gentleman in every way. Her image of herself was completely opposite.

She wrote once, ". . .I prayed with all my heart that the ugly, pigeon-toed little girl, whose crooked back obliged her to walk with her head held very much upon one side, would never be pointed out to anyone as the daughter of this fine man."

When Jane was eight, her father remarried. The new union brought Jane a stepbrother, George, who was about her own age. Together the two children played games and shared laughter. George helped provide Jane with confidence and poise. But she still enjoyed those wonderful times when she could be with her father alone.

One day Mr. Addams took Jane on a buggy ride. As they rode along narrow streets in a poor section of town, Jane looked sadly at the houses wedged closely together. Dust drifted in the air and unpleasant smells coated the breezes.

"What a horrid place to live!" Jane burst out. "There is no room to play—or to grow a garden. How could anyone live in these tiny little houses?"

"It is all these people can afford," Mr. Addams answered. "It is the best they can do."

Jane's mind wandered to her own home, a ten room brick house surrounded by pine trees along the Cedar River. Again her heart saddened at the sights and smells around her.

"Someday," she said softly, "I am going to live in a very large house. But it will not be built among other large houses. It will be built among tiny houses like these. And I will welcome everyone who wants to come to my house."

Mr. Addams smiled, snapping the reins lightly. "Maybe you will, Jennie. Maybe you will."

Jane enjoyed going to school, quickly and firmly choosing English and Latin as her favorite subjects. At seventeen, she entered Rockford Seminary, a simple, hard-working school where students did their own chores and cleaned their own rooms. The curriculum of ancient history, literature, languages, natural science and philosophy was structured within the framework of strong Christian doctrine.

Friends and good grades came easily to Jane at Rockford. Her classmates elected her class president and she captured honors as valedictorian at graduation. But inwardly, Jane was troubled. She knew she wanted to do something meaningful with her life—but what? Her classmates urged her to become a missionary like many of them had chosen to do. No, Jane did not feel inclined toward missionary work.

"There must be something else," she told a classmate Ellen Starr. "I just haven't found it."

Still uncertain, Jane decided to enroll at the Women's Medical College in Philadelphia. Perhaps, just perhaps, this might be the answer. "Doctor Jane Addams" had a nice sound to it!

The death of her father when Jane was twenty-one left her troubled and confused. Her unhappiness was deepened by a painful back problem which forced her to have an operation and stay in bed for six months.

Jane's doctor offered firm advice. "When you are better, you should travel, see the world. Surely you would love Europe with all its art galleries and museums."

The doctor's words sounded refreshing and exciting. So Jane and a group of her friends set sail for Europe in 1883.

For a brief time, the parties and sightseeing trips thrust Jane into a world of happy spirits and fun. But soon she began to yearn for something else—something she could dedicate herself to, a task to which she could devote her energy and time.

One night a friend of Jane's suggested a tour of one of the poorer parts of London.

"It's where I've been working, doing missionary work," she explained. "There's so much to do."

Jane quickly saw what her friend meant. The streets of London's East End were cluttered with drunken derelicts and castaways. The stench of rotting garbage was everywhere, mingling with the thick smog and chimney smoke.

Stopping to watch a vegetable auction, Jane could not believe what she saw. The sellers had obtained their vegetables at the regular London markets—vegetables that had been judged too spoiled or rotten for sale. But here, in the East End, starving people begged for battered heads of lettuce and bruised tomatoes.

"Look at their clothing," one of Jane's friends whispered. "It's so torn and filthy."

But Jane was not looking at what the people wore.

16

Instead she watched their hands, their empty and work-worn hands, reaching out for food unfit to eat.

That scene in London was one Jane knew she would never forget. Inside of her a fire was lit. The flames of that fire spread quickly as Jane continued her travels. Wherever she visited, in cities of Europe or in the United States, Jane toured the slum areas. Carefully she looked for ways of helping the poor and friendless.

A delightful surprise awaited Jane when she returned to London's East End on a later visit. A man named Samuel Barnett had opened a "settlement house" called Toynbee Hall. Students from Oxford and Cambridge Universities "settled" in Toynbee Hall to work with people in the poor neighborhoods. The students formed clubs and held discussions. The people in the East End knew they were welcome visitors at Toynbee Hall.

"It works so well in London," Jane told her good friend Ellen Starr. "Could it not work in Chicago? There are so many people there who need help, who crave friendship and understanding."

"But—but it is easier for a man to do such things," Ellen answered.

Jane's eyes blazed with determination. "It makes it a bigger challenge for us then," she snapped back. "And it will be all the greater accomplishment when we complete the job."

Ellen nodded her agreement. Eagerly Jane returned to Chicago, hopeful of putting her idea into action. First she needed to find just the right place for a settlement house.

In fifty years Chicago's population had grown from a mere seven thousand to over one million people. There had been little time for careful city planning. Slum areas stretched for miles in some parts of Chicago. Most of them were packed with people born in foreign countries. Suspicious of those who did not speak their language or follow their customs, these immigrants struggled through their daily lives.

Days became weeks as Jane searched for the location she wanted. She talked to missionaries and reporters. Carefully she explained her goals.

"We want to open a house where people can come, share a meal, laugh and enjoy themselves," Jane said. "Too many people live their lives without ever knowing joy and love."

Not everyone accepted Jane's ideas.

"Women living alone in a slum neighborhood! Ridiculous!" blurted one newspaper reporter. "You will be robbed, perhaps murdered!"

"No one should live in a slum unless he has to!" was another opinion expressed. "Enjoy the money your father left you, don't waste it!"

But Jane was determined. Finally, in the late summer of 1889, her long search ended. Sitting among a cluster of old tenements on the corner of Polk and Halsted was a dilapidated brick building. On one side was a saloon and on the other, a funeral parlor. Once the home of Charles J. Hull, a rich Chicago businessman, the house sat falling apart.

"It's perfect!" Jane told Ellen. "Let's get to work."

Not a moment was wasted. Quickly the leaks in the roof were patched up and cracks in the ceilings plastered. Jane and Ellen polished the rich oak floors until they shined. They scraped the ugly paint off the white marble fireplaces. Slowly the house returned to the beautiful mansion it had once been.

Finally, the work was done. Jane was sure people in the neighborhood would flock into the beautiful house, eager to enjoy parties and fun. But it didn't happen.

"I think I know our mistake," she told Ellen one morning. "We should not expect these people to mingle with each other at once. What can a Greek man say to an Italian man if they do not speak the same language? How can Russian women talk with Mexican women? No, we must bring people together slowly."

In the days that followed, Jane and Ellen visited the neighborhood markets. They talked to everyone they met.

"Perhaps you would like to visit us Tuesday night," Jane told a group of Greek women. "We are going to sing Greek songs."

"Friday evening we will be having games at our house," said Ellen to a group of boys one afternoon. "Why don't you come?"

Slowly people came, first out of curiosity, then because they had enjoyed themselves. Factory girls stopped for a cup of tea after work. Jane told the children stories. Plays were performed. Classes in drawing were started. Before long, two thousand people a week were visiting Hull House.

News of Hull House spread throughout the city. Jane was asked to give speeches about her work. She accepted, hoping people with money would help support Hull House.

Her plan worked. Donations for food, coal, medicine and clothing poured in. There were dozens of ways to spend each dollar—and Jane saw that not a penny was wasted.

Children always found a special place in Jane's heart. At Christmastime, she helped them make special decorations and presents for their parents. She was never too busy to sew up a torn trouser or nurse a scratched elbow.

One night, as Jane was eating supper, there was a knock on the door. A trembling woman burst into the room.

"My boy, my boy is home with fever. He say he want da Americana lady. You come?"

Quickly Jane slipped into a coat and followed the woman to her tiny Italian home. A small body shivered under a heavy quilt in the bedroom.

Jane silently sat down beside the bed. She covered the boy's hand with her own. The boy's eyes opened and he smiled.

"Nice Americana lady," he whispered. "Nice—"

Still smiling, the dying boy closed his eyes. He had seen his good friend for the last time. No longer was he afraid. Jane sat beside his bed.

As the years passed, new buildings were added to Hull House. A gym, an art gallery, a theatre, workshops, classrooms—all sprang from the needs of the people, Jane's people.

And as the work of Hull House flourished, visitors came from all over the world. They sought ideas for starting settlement houses and programs in their own countries.

In 1931 Jane Addams shared the Nobel Peace Prize with the president of Columbia University. The judges said Jane "had shown by love and kindness that people can share all that is good in the human spirit."

On May 21, 1935, Jane Addams died in Chicago. A simple ceremony was held at Hull House. The rich and famous, the poor and unknown, stood side-by-side. They had come to pay their final respects to a woman who had reminded them to "love thy neighbor as thyself."

*   *   *

BIBLIOGRAPHY (Addams)

Addams, Jane. TWENTY YEARS AT HULL HOUSE. New York: The MacMillan Company, 1924.

Ames, Noel. THESE WONDERFUL PEOPLE. Chicago: Peoples Book Club, 1947.

Judson, Clara Ingram. CITY NEIGHBOR: THE STORY OF JANE ADDAMS. New York: Charles Scribner's Sons, 1951.

Large, Laura Antoinette. LITTLE KNOWN STORIES OF WELL-KNOWN AMERICANS. New York: Platt and Munk, Inc., 1935.

Linn, James Weber. JANE ADDAMS, A BIOGRAPHY. New York: Appleton-Century, Inc., 1935.

Keller, Gail Faithful. JANE ADDAMS. New York: Thomas Crowell, Inc., 1951.

Meigs, Cornelia. JANE ADDAMS. New York: Little, Brown and Company, 1970.

Peterson, Helen S. JANE ADDAMS. Champaign, Illinois: Garrard Publishing Company, 1965.

Wise, Winifred E. JANE ADDAMS OF HULL HOUSE. New York: Harcourt, Brace and World, Inc., 1935.

MARY ANN BICKERDYKE
1817-1901

"What in tarnation is going on in this barn?"

At the sound of her grandfather's voice, eight-year-old Mary Ann Ball turned around. In her hands she gently held a small black crow.

"I think she's ready to leave," the girl answered as she stroked the bird's back. "I took off the splint and her arm seems just fine."

Grandpa Rodgers rubbed his chin. "Sounds like her voice is good and strong too. Those neighbors on the next farm could hear that little crow's caw."

Mary Ann led the way out of the barn into the warm sunlight. Opening her hands, she watched the crow gain its balance. Moments later the bird leaped into the air. Around the barnyard flew the crow, swooping and drifting with the light summer breeze. Then, with a final bow, the bird disappeared beyond the trees.

"I'll miss her," Mary Ann said softly.

"That little creature owes you its life," Grandpa announced. "If I ever take sick, I know who I'll be asking to nurse me—that is, if she's not too busy caring for a sick cow or squirrel."

Mary laughed, her long brown braids dancing. She hugged her grandfather and then ran toward the farmhouse. It was almost time to set the table for dinner.

There was always much work to be done on the Ohio farm where Mary Ann lived with her grandparents. Born July 19, 1817, Mary Ann was only seventeen months old when her mother died. Soon afterwards, Mary Ann's father went away. The young girl was given to her grandparents to raise.

"I watched you let the crow loose," Grandma Rodgers said, scooping up the small piles of peas she had finished shelling. "Looks like that broken wing mended right fine."

Mary Ann nodded as she set the wooden plates on the table. "It's fun helping animals. It makes me feel good inside. I'm glad we live on a farm where there are so many animals to take care of."

Farm living ended for Mary Ann when she was sixteen. The death of her grandparents caused the farm to be sold. She traveled to Oberlin to live with an uncle. Soon she began working for a professor who invited Mary Ann to sit in on classes at a new college that had opened in the town.

"A woman today should be educated," the professor insisted. "Do not listen to those who feel a college education is only for men."

Mary Ann's attendance in classes stopped when she moved to Cincinnati to live with her Uncle Henry. But a new interest developed after Mary Ann met a house painter named Robert Bickerdyke.

A widower with three small children, Robert Bicker-dyke was a lonely man. He found comfort in music, spending many hours playing instruments for dances, and demonstrating them at music stores. For hours Mary Ann sat listening to Robert strum a banjo, or tinkle the keys of a piano.

"I'm thinking there's more interest in Robert than his music," Uncle Henry often teased.

Blushing, Mary Ann always shook her head. But when Robert proposed, all blushes were put aside beneath a white wedding veil. In 1847 Mary Ann and Robert were married.

One night after supper, Mary stood beside the piano listening to Robert play. Quietly she hummed along, now and then singing a few lines of a familiar tune.

After an hour, Robert stopped and removed a letter from his coat pocket. "This is from my brother," he said, handing the piece of paper to Mary Ann. "Read it, and tell me what you think."

As her husband again began to play, Mary read the letter carefully. Robert's brother wanted them to move west, to a small town named Galesburg, Illinois. Mary Ann thought about the idea. It was a decision not to be quickly made. There were Robert's three children to think of, as well as one Mary Ann was expecting in three months. Yet the thought was exciting. Illinois was said to be a growing state, where land was plentiful and fairly priced.

"What is your thinking on the matter?" Robert asked.

Mary smiled. "I'm thinking it might be quite an adventure. If you be willing, I am."

So it was that the Bickerdyke clan headed west and found a new home in Galesburg. House painting jobs were many, and the evenings with the growing family offered fun and pleasure. Mary Ann became a mother twice in Galesburg, with sons James and Hiram.

Then came tragedy. One morning Robert could not get out of bed. A doctor was summoned, but by nightfall Robert's condition worsened. During the night he died, the victim of an unknown illness.

There were few business opportunities available for a widow with young children to support. Mary Ann made use of her past skills. On her grandparents' farm and at her uncle's home, she had learned much about the healing qualities of fruits and herbs, the value of fresh air and clean water. Soon Mary Ann was busy caring for the sick in Galesburg, being ready to answer a call for help whenever needed.

In other parts of the country, discontent was brewing between northern and southern states. Mary Ann was delighted when another Illinoisian, Abraham Lincoln, was elected President.

"Surely Mr. Lincoln will find solutions to the country's problems," she wrote to a friend. "I heard him when he debated Mr. Douglas here in Galesburg. Mr. Lincoln is a right honorable man."

But Lincoln's "right and honor" could not curb the anger and unrest felt by many Americans. In April of 1861, cannon exploded. The United States was at war!

President Lincoln issued a quick call for volunteers. Over five hundred men responded from Galesburg.

In the weeks that followed, reports of the dead and injured alarmed the people of Galesburg. No one had thought the fighting would last. But the lists of casualties grew longer.

One morning Mary Ann sat in a Galesburg church. For weeks she had helped collect money and supplies for an army hospital south in Cairo, Illinois. A meeting had been called to decide the person who could deliver the donations.

"It must be someone efficient, trustworthy and unafraid," said the minister. "It must also be someone who will make sure our money and supplies reach those who need it most. Generals and military leaders do not always welcome help from outside the army."

"Or they sometimes take donated money for themselves!" exclaimed a voice from the rear of the church.

A woman at the front rose. "I know who would get our donations through to the right people—Mary Ann Bickerdyke!"

Mary flushed as people turned to look at her. But their heads were nodding agreement, and others soon voiced their support.

"Would you be willing to go?" the minister asked.

For a long moment Mary Ann did not speak. She still had two children at home to care for. Also, it was a dangerous task, one which she had never expected. But this was war—and maybe she could make a personal contribution.

"I'll go," she answered, rising to her feet. "If you people will look after my boys, I can go with a clear conscience. It's the Lord's work you're asking me to do, and when I'm doing the work of the Lord, I shall see it's done properly."

The next day a freight car was loaded with the supplies and Mary set out for Cairo, Illinois. When she arrived, she supervised the unloading. One of the soldiers who had helped unload the cargo from Galesburg stepped forward.

"We'll take the supplies with us to camp," he offered.

Mary Ann Shook her head. "Thank you kindly, but I am under strict orders to deliver these supplies to Dr.

Woodward. He is from Galesburg and wrote us requesting help."

Again and again soldiers asked to take the supplies with them. Standing in black Shaker bonnet and grey calico dress under the hot June sun, Mary Ann stood firm. Orders she had—and orders she would obey.

When Dr. Woodward finally arrived, Mary Ann was still standing beside the supplies she had brought.

"I-I'm so sorry you were kept waiting," the doctor apologized. "We had five more wounded men brought into our camp just when I was leaving to come here. I imagine you have had no easy time keeping these supplies from others. The station is watched carefully by many people. When hospital supplies arrive, everyone tries to get them."

Mary Ann nodded. "Yes, there <u>have</u> been many wanting to cart these things off. But no one asked twice."

Listening to Mary Ann's firm voice and strict manner, Doctor Woodward could easily understand. There was no question that Mary Ann Bickerdyke was a woman who knew just what she was doing and how to do it.

Not a moment was wasted when Mary Ann reached Doctor Woodward's hospital tents. Two men shared each narrow cot—flies buzzed around water buckets—dirty straw served as beds for many of the injured.

"Get me some men to help clean this place!" Mary Ann told Doctor Woodward. "These soldiers would have a better chance of survival on the battlefield than in here."

"But, Miss Bickerdyke! You were not sent here to—"

But Mary Ann was not listening. Already she was starting to carry out piles of dirty straw. Warily Doctor Woodward turned away and left to round up help.

Quickly the men were moved outside the hospital tents. The cots were stripped and Mary Ann used fresh linen she brought to recover them. Hot water was boiled for baths.

"Before any man gets back inside a tent, he must have a hot bath or scrubbing," she announced.

Again Doctor Woodward protested. "They can't bathe in the open air."

"I don't know why in tarnation they can't. In fact, they must! Have your men help those who can't bathe themselves. Here's some fresh yellow soap I brought. And I'll have clean nightclothes ready for them when they've finished washing."

Reluctantly the doctor gave in. Within hours the job was done. Inside the orderly hospital tents rested the injured.

Once she had seen what work needed to be done, Mary Ann gave up all thoughts of returning to Galesburg. Her children were in good hands, and there was much work to be done with the war effort.

"You take care of my two boys, Lord," Mary Ann prayed each night, "and I shall try to care for as many of yours as I can."

As Mary Ann traveled from hospital tent to battlefield, the injured soldiers welcomed her warmly. "You're just like my mother," one boy said. Before long, Mary Ann carried a beloved nickname among all the wounded soldiers she met—"Mother Bickerdyke."

But Mary Ann was not so warmly welcomed by generals and doctors. Her quick sharp tongue, coupled with her immediate commands, gained her little favor among the hospital supervisors.

One doctor called Mary Ann a "cyclone in calico." He complained angrily to the general in charge of the hospital.

"This Bickerdyke woman has no authority to do what

she is doing. She is not really trained as a nurse."

The general summoned Mary Ann and explained the doctor's charges. Mary Ann turned red.

"That doctor is a contract surgeon. He looks closely after his private patients, those who have plenty of money and will pay him richly. He seldom looks in on the soldiers as he is also paid to do."

The general listened, and allowed Mary Ann to continue her work.

Weeks turned into months, then years, as the Civil War fighting continued. Mary Ann was always ready to travel at a moment's notice. Wherever there were wounded soldiers, she wanted to be. The job to be done did not matter. Whether it be cooking, cleaning, scrubbing, rolling bandages, helping at surgical operations— no task was too unimportant.

"I feel valuable," she wrote home. "I know the doctors still resent me—last evening one called me a meddlesome, blabbering old magpie—but it is the boys I am serving, as well as the Lord."

As often as she could, Mary Ann returned to Galesburg. She missed her own two sons and enjoyed the times she could be with them. But soon the desire to return to the wounded grew too strong and off she would go again.

Finally, the Civil War ended. Soldiers returned to their homes. Mary Ann paid a last visit to hospitals where she had served. Satisfied the job had been finished, Mary Ann headed home to Galesburg.

But it was soon clear that she was needed again. Soldiers who had fought in the war were entitled to pensions. Somehow the pension program became a tangled jigsaw puzzle in Washington. Mary Ann joined the fight for the benefits the soldiers rightly deserved. She still thought of them as "her boys" and she would not stop helping them until they were given their proper rewards.

The soldiers "Mother Bickerdyke" tended during the war often came to visit her. Even as the years slowed her step and kept her from traveling, Mary Ann was always eager to welcome her guests.

Mary Ann spent her final years living with her son Jimmy in Kansas. She died peacefully in her sleep on November 8, 1901.

Mary Ann was buried beside her husband in Galesburg's Linwood Cemetery. A large statue, sculptured by Theo Alice Ruggles-Kitson, was erected in the city square—a statue depicting "Mother Bickerdyke" kneeling beside a wounded soldier and holding a cup of water to his lips.

soldier upon viewing the statue. "She would have liked that."

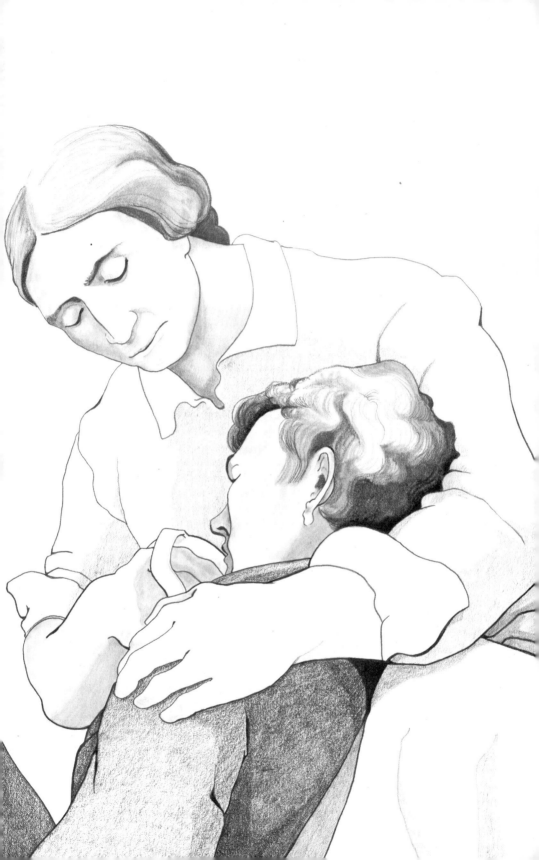

*　　*　　*

BIBLIOGRAPHY (Bickerdyke)

Baker, Nina Brown. CYCLONE IN CALICO. Boston: Little, Brown and Company, 1952.

Chase, Julia A. MARY A. BICKERDYKE, "MOTHER". Lawrence, Kansas: Journal Publishing House, 1896.

Davis, Margaret Burton. MOTHER BICKERDYKE AND THE SOLDIERS. San Francisco: A. T. Dewey, 1886.

DeLeeuw, Adele. CIVIL WAR NURSE: MARY ANN BICKERDYKE. New York: Julian Messner, Inc., 1973.

Kellogg, Florence. MOTHER BICKERDYKE AS I KNEW HER. Chicago: Unity Publishing Company, 1907.

Livermore, Mary Ashton Rice. MY STORY OF THE WAR. Hartford: A. D. Worthington and Company, 1887.

Livermore, Mary Ashton Rice. THE STORY OF MY LIFE. Hartford: A. D. Worthington and Company, 1897.

Wright, Helen and Samuel Rapport (editors). GREAT ADVENTURES IN NURSING. New York: Harper and Brothers, 1960.

MARGUERITE (MARGRET) BROOKS
1896-1982

Margret gripped her mother's hand tightly. The seven year old girl gazed saucer-eyed at the tall ceilings, wide halls and long hallways of the old building.

"Here it is," Mrs. Brooks whispered, leading her daughter into a hospital room numbered 207.

At the sight of her father's smiling face, Margret rushed into his open arms. She felt safe and secure inside the man's giant hug.

"What a delightful young visitor!" August Brooks declared, patting Margret's auburn curls. "I've been waiting for this moment all day."

Margret slowly backed away, looking over the hospital bed on which her father lay. An infection had diseased Mr. Brooks' leg so badly that it had to be amputated. Just the thought of it caused Margret's eyes to cloud with tears.

"Did you go to the concert in Moline yesterday?" Mr.

Brooks asked.

"Oh, yes, Papa," Margret answered. "It was wonderful. The mayor of Rock Island was there, too, sitting with the mayor of Moline. The music was beautiful!"

"And are you prepared for your lesson tomorrow?"

"I'll be ready, Papa. I've been practicing."

Katherine Brooks smiled at her daughter. "Yes, your little girl practiced right through her time for doing the dishes last evening, August. Thankfully, her three older brothers agreed to help."

Margret flushed. She promised that she would do something special for Fredrick, Walter and Augustan when she got home.

"Well, Doctor Allen has a surprise for you. I told him what good care you gave me before I came into the hospital. He promised he would give you a complete tour of the hospital."

"And I never break my promises!"

Margret whirled around to see a man in the doorway. He wore a white physician's uniform. The gentleman motioned Margret forward.

For the next hour, Doctor Allen led the young girl through the hospital hallways. Margret was fascinated. There were so many things to see. Every room boasted a different number or sign. Men and women walked briskly, carrying out their duties. They always smiled and spoke pleasantly to Doctor Allen.

"We won't be going into the operating rooms," explained Doctor Allen. "But this one is where your father had his surgery. He is making a good recovery."

Margret nodded, intrigued by the two men entering the room. They wore unusual masks, surgical coverings, to prevent any germs from their bodies spreading into the patient's.

Before she went home, Margret was given a special present from Doctor Allen. It was a jar of ether.

"I like the smell," the girl exclaimed.

"Not everyone does," the doctor laughed. "It's not exactly a favorite perfume around here."

When Mr. Brooks came home from the hospital, Margret took much care to see that he was comfortable. Often she spent hours playing the piano for him.

By the time she graduated from the Immaculate Conception Conservatory of Music, Margret was an accomplished pianist, harpist and organist. She assumed the name Marguerite for personal reasons.

With her father's encouragement, as well as the good wishes of Doctor Allen and Doctor M. S. Dondanville of Moline, Marguerite headed to Chicago where she enrolled in the St. Joseph's Hospital School of Nursing. It was a superior institution with the best of facilities and training.

Marguerite liked Chicago. She decided to do her postgraduate work at Cook County Hospital. When she was done, she accepted positions as operating room supervisor at St. Joseph's and later at the Central School of Nursing at the University of Minnesota in Minneapolis.

But Marguerite missed home, her family and the Quad City area. In 1930, she accepted the job of operating room supervisor at Moline Public Hospital. Three years later, she was named administrator of the entire hospital.

Marguerite enjoyed her new job. But there were others who grumbled and complained.

"It's too big of a responsibility for a woman," one hospital board member said.

"She won't last a year," agreed another.

Marguerite knew there were people unhappy with a woman getting such an important position. There was only one thing to do — prove that she *was* the right choice.

It wasn't easy. Not only did some doubt her abilities as woman but others made unkind remarks about her Catholic faith.

"We'll probably have statues at the end of every hall soon," Marguerite overheard a doctor tell a nurse one day.

"Not unless you choose to put them there," the new administrator quietly remarked.

Carefully Marguerite planned the future for Moline Public Hospital. Doctors like M.S. and L.A. Dondanville helped her, as did Dr. H. M. Gibson and Dr. Silvio Errico. Her quiet but efficient manner began to win her many friends and supporters. Soon she was able to turn her attention completely to hospital problems.

One of her first major goals was to make Moline Public Hospital self-supporting. For years it had cost the tax-payers a great deal of money to keep it operating. By providing a new budget, Marguerite set up a program by which the hospital could make money. By 1946, Moline Hospital was completely self-supporting.

But even more important than the financial end of running a hospital was the day-to-day personal care of the patients. She felt deep disappointment whenever the nurses or doctors at Moline Public were criticized.

"We must never forget that we exist for the well being of the sick," she frequently reminded those on her staff. "We must set aside all of our personal troubles the minute we come on duty. Our sole concern must be the proper health care of our patients."

The Moline Public Hospital School of Nursing became known nationwide for its fine training and friendly spirit. While Marguerite was hospital director, 1,165 student nurses were graduated. She helped establish the School of X-Ray Technology, which graduated another 110 trained technicians, while her Operating Room Technician Course produced another 100 graduates.

When Moline's Black Hawk College expressed an interest in working with the hospital, Marguerite Brooks was instrumental in setting up a program. Under her guidance, the hospital provided clinical experiences in medical-surgical nursing, obstetrics and recovery room techniques for students in the practical nursing program and others from Black Hawk College.

"We need more room," hospital directors moaned.

"Maybe we're trying to do too much," cautioned another.

"We must be ready to meet the health needs of the community," Marguerite declared. "We must be ready to grow."

Grow Moline Public Hospital did. Bed capacity mushroomed from 100 to 275. She supervised the building of sixteen new structures with a total price tag of over $15,000,000. Eighteen new departments were added in the health-care fields. A trauma center was begun. In 1940, she led the way for Blue Cross medical plans in the community.

"Her desk was covered with ongoing programs," noted one co-worker, "but Miss Brooks always knew where everything was."

She knew who people were, too. She often walked down hospital hallways, calling staff members by name. She enjoyed popping in on patients, sharing a cheery, encouraging word or two.

Doctors on the staff of Moline Public received special attention. When she retired in 1977, after 47 years of service at the hospital, she noted how much she would miss "my boys. All the physicians were my boys, and as

40

the older doctors retired or moved on, there were always the young ones moving in to take their places, needing my guidance."

Many honors came to Marguerite Brooks for her services as chief administrator of Moline Public Hospital. National, state and area nurses' organizations elected her to top offices and named her "Woman of the Year." Businesswomen named her "Boss of the Year" and "Chief Executive of the Year."

After her retirement, Marguerite was able to do many of the things she had little time for while she was working. She enjoyed listening to music, reading, and collecting figurines. She entertained her nieces and nephews, thrilling to their fond label of "Aunt Marney."

One afternoon, Marguerite returned to the hospital she had served so long and so well. Dignitaries gathered to dedicate the Marguerite N. Brooks Learning Resource Center and Laboratory, a new two million dollar facility.

"I'm so honored and flattered," Miss Brooks exclaimed. "You have made me very proud."

But the last sunsets were approaching. For her final illness, Marguerite returned to the hospital she had served. On May 26, 1982, she died.

"A grand woman is gone," noted one newspaper editorial. "She was a blessing to her entire community. We shall miss her, but the work she accomplished will live long after her. Thank you, Miss Brooks."

*   *   *

BIBLIOGRAPHY (BROOKS)

Baraks, Gloria and co-authors. PROFILES IN LEADERSHIP. Rock Island: Quest Publications, 1981.

Quad City Times. "Marguerite N. Brooks, Obituary." Davenport, Iowa: Lee Enterprises, May 26, 1982.

LORRAINE HANSBERRY
1930-1965

"It isn't fair! It just isn't fair!"

Eight-year-old Lorraine Hansberry kicked at a small pile of snow on the sidewalk as she walked home from school. A single tear slid down her cold cheek. Lorraine wiped it off with a yellow mitten. She slowed her steps as she approached her house.

Glancing across the street, Lorraine watched several children building a snowman. They were laughing and playing. One tossed a snowball at another. Again they all laughed.

Suddenly one of the boys in the group spotted Lorraine. He stopped and pointed. "Hey, why don't you get out of our neighborhood? We don't want you people around here!"

"Yeah, move out!" one of his companions yelled. "Nobody wants you black people here!"

Lorraine stepped quickly to her front door as she

looked back at the barrage of snowballs hurled at her. Quietly she slipped inside the front door and tugged off her boots. She listened for a moment. There was no sound. Maybe no one was home. But just as Lorraine stood up —

"Lorraine? Lor-raine? Is that you, baby?"

The sound of her mother's voice halted Lorraine. The girl took off her coat. "Yes, Mama."

"Go on into the kitchen, dear. There's some hot cocoa on the stove to warm you up."

"Thanks, Mama." Slowly the girl walked to the kitchen and poured herself a cup of the cocoa. It *did* taste good. But cocoa could do little to soothe Lorraine's feelings.

"Say, where's a bright smile for your Mama?" Nannie Hansberry appeared at the kitchen doorway and wiped her hands on her apron.

Usually Lorraine could force a smile, but not today. She looked woefully up at her mother. "Isn't anyone else here?"

Mrs. Hansberry shook her head. "Your father is showing a client some property. Looks like a good prospect for a sale. Your brother, Carl Jr., had basketball practice and Perry went to see about getting a newspaper route. Sister Jamie is babysitting."

Lorraine sipped the hot cocoa. Her mother moved behind her chair and softly rubbed her back. "Bad day at school again, hon?" Mrs. Hansberry asked.

Lorraine did not answer immediately. She had shared so often that it seemed so useless. Every day at school was the same thing. Kids made fun of her, often chasing her home after classes were over.

"It will get better," her mother promised. "You will learn to love your new home."

But things did not get better. Although the Hansberrys' new home had its own lawn and trees, Lorraine did not like it. She longed for the days when they lived on the South Side. Though the buildings were old, the streets dirty and dangerous, at least the people were black. Lorraine had friends, real friends. If only her father could understand. . .

Yet Carl Augustus Hansberry seemed to live in his own world. He worked hard at his real estate business and founded one of the first banks for Negroes in Chicago. He wanted the best for his family, and he was happy to move them out of the South Side. No longer would they live among old three-and-four story tenements with their crumbling walls. Their new home was perfect for one-family dwelling — perfect for everyone but Lorraine.

Ever since she was born on May 19, 1930, Lorraine knew no one but Chicago relatives and friends in the city's South Side. Now she was surrounded by white people. Her new neighbors did not like having a black family move into their all-white neighborhood.

"This is a free country," Mr. Hansberry said often. "We can live where we please."

Mr. Hansberry's neighbors did not agree. They decided that none of them would sell a home to a black family. The agreement was called a restrictive covenant. But Carl Hansberry knew Illinois law and fought for the right to buy a house where he wished. He took the case to court.

For six years, judges discussed the case. It finally went all the way to the Supreme Court of the United States.

While the judges argued, Lorraine and her family suffered. There were cruel phone calls at all hours, rocks thrown at their house and garbage heaped on the lawn. Sometimes Lorraine and her sister, Mamie, lay awake as their older brothers stood guard at the windows and their mother and father slept downstairs near the front and back doors.

During the day there were the insults and threats, the boys pulling her hair and the girls slapping her. Often she came home in tears.

"Oh, why can't people just leave us alone?" the girl moaned.

Carl Hansberry would not give up the fight. Finally, the decision came. The Supreme Court ruled a family had the right to live wherever they wished.

But it was an empty victory. Mr. Hansberry felt bitter toward America. The court case had cost him much of the family savings. The new house had brought much unhappiness.

"We're moving," he told his family one day. "We're going to Mexico City where the color of one's skin is not important."

Everyone was surprised, especially Lorraine. She was a freshman at Englewood High School in Chicago. Mexico City seemed like another world, such a faraway place.

But the Hansberry family did *not* move to Mexico City. While completing his business affairs, Carl Hansberry suddenly suffered a cerebral hemorrhage and died.

Lorraine felt angry and bitter. She vowed that someday, somehow, she would fight against racial prejudice as her father had done.

High school days were filled with activity and excitement. Lorraine showed a talent for art and dreamed of someday being an illustrator or designer. She spent hours sketching and drawing.

Despite her interest in art, it was English class that captured Lorraine's mind. She fell in love with Shakespeare, thrilling to every speech in "Othello," "Romeo and Juliet" and "Hamlet." The theatre and plays held a special magic that left the high school girl breathless. When she and her classmates attended a Chicago production of "Dark of the Moon," Lorraine left the theatre convinced that somehow she wanted to be a part of this exciting world.

Following her graduation from Englewood High in 1948, Lorraine enrolled at the University of Wisconsin. She declared herself an art major.

But once again it was the theatre that demanded her interest and attention. Strindberg, Ibsen and other playwrights made the world spring to life on stage. "Juno and the Paycock," a play by Sean O'Casey, depicted life in an old Dublin tenement and left a memorable mark on Lorraine's mind.

At the Art Institute of Chicago, Roosevelt College and in Guadalajara, Mexico, Lorraine tried to find her art talent. She became convinced there was none. The urge to write grew stronger. Hearing that most writers got their start in New York, she found herself an apartment in Greenwich Village. To support herself, she worked for Mae and Motya Nemiroff as a restaurant waitress.

One day Robert Nemiroff came into the restaurant to visit his parents. A song writer and music publisher, Robert shared exciting stories about the business of writing. Lorraine was fascinated. She had been working on a few short stories and plays, but she knew she had much to learn.

"I'll help you," Robert offered.

It was not only writing interests that drew Robert to Lorraine. Her bright eyes and smile, her quick sense of humor, her sensitive spirit — all contributed. In 1953, Lorraine and Robert were married.

In the years that followed, Lorraine struggled to become a good writer. But she was afraid to submit any of

48

her work to publishers. It just wasn't good enough, she told herself. Only quality work found its way into print.

One night Lorraine and Robert went to a Broadway play. It was about a Negro family, but Lorraine was disappointed.

"The characters just weren't real," she told her husband as they drove home. "I could write a better play than that."

"Then do it?" Robert declared. "Don't just talk about it. Do it!"

Lorraine accepted the challenge. For the next year she dedicated herself to writing a play. She wrote from her own experience, her own life. The play was about a black family from the South Side of Chicago who wanted to leave their tenement and buy a new home in a better neighborhood. Sometimes when Robert came home, he found Lorraine in tears. The sadness of her childhood haunted her. But it gave her power and feeling in her writing. When the play was finished, she called it "A Raisin in the Sun," which came from a poem written by black poet Langston Hughes.

Robert was proud of Lorraine. Yet she was afraid to send her completed play to a publisher. One night after dinner, Robert persuaded her to read the play to their guests. Lorraine reluctantly agreed. When she finished, her friends applauded. One of them, Phillip Rose, claimed, "I want to produce your play on Broadway."

Lorraine was thrilled. "I suddenly realized the play had taken on a life of its own," she recalled.

Lorraine learned quickly that putting a play together was not easy. It required money and time. A theatre had to be rented, actors and a director hired, sets and scenery designed. But as each step moved the play closer to presentation, Lorraine grew more eager to see the production. She was happy when her good friend, Sidney Poitier, was selected to play the leading role of Walter Lee Younger.

"A Raisin in the Sun" opened in New Haven, Connecticut. It was an instant success.

"Hansberry combines humor and drama with just the proper touch," wrote one critic. "Broadway audiences can look forward to a theatrical treat."

Despite the cheerful tryouts in New Haven, Philadelphia and Chicago, Lorraine still worried about Broadway. Never had there been a Broadway play written by a Negro woman. Lorraine feared the failure of her work might harm the image of her entire race.

Her fears were wasted. "A Raisin in the Sun" proved a top hit which brought the audience to its feet at the final curtain. Seated in the front row between her mother and husband, Lorraine soaked in the thunderous applause.

"Thank you, Papa," she whispered to herself.

"A Raisin in the Sun" won the New York Drama Critics Award for 1959, defeating productions penned by such noted playwrights as Archibald MacLeish, Eugene O'Neill and Tennessee Williams. Lorraine had truly made theatre history.

Newspaper reporters wrote stories about Lorraine. She was a guest on radio and television programs. Interviewers always seemed to comment on her dark, brown eyes and her soft spoken voice.

"You'll probably be changing your life a great deal now," noted one TV hostess. "You'll be wanting a housekeeper and cook."

Lorraine laughed. "Oh, no, I won't. Maybe my life has changed some, but I'm still the same person."

True to her word, Lorraine did not change. Although royalties from "A Raisin in the Sun" climbed to $3000 a

NOW PLAYING!

A Raisin in the Sun

by
LORRAINE
HANSBERRY

week, Lorraine and Robert kept their small Greenwich Village apartment above Joe's Hand Laundry. Whenever they could, they took off on short skiing trips and went to the theatre.

Before the success of "A Raisin in the Sun," Lorraine had been hesitant about sharing her writing. That attitude *did* change. She planned to write a novel, short stories, even an opera. But first she would write another play. She titled it "The Sign in Sidney Brustein's Window."

Soon after beginning her new play, Lorraine began having pains in her stomach. She tried to ignore them but finally they grew so intense, she went to the doctor. He diagnosed her illness as ulcers.

"So that's what a little success brings," Lorraine chuckled. "Well, I'll have to slow down a bit."

Slowing down did not seem to help. Still Lorraine managed to complete the play before entering the hospital for tests.

Each day cast members of "The Sign in Sidney Brustein's Window" stopped by to visit.

On opening night for "The Sign in Sidney Brustein's Window," Lorraine sat in the front row. The date was October 14, 1964. Once again she listened to the audience applaud her efforts. She squeezed Robert's hand, enjoying the thrill of the evening.

But Lorraine's illness was much more serious than the doctors had thought. What had been diagnosed as ulcers turned out to be cancer. On January 12, 1965, Lorraine Hansberry died.

"So great a talent to be lost so early," wrote one theatre critic. "At thirty-four, Lorraine Hansberry was already a major playwright who could create characters of great depth and power. We all suffer from this young woman's early exit from the stage of life."

*　　　*　　　*

BIBLIOGRAPHY (HANSBERRY)

Current Biography. LORRAINE HANSBERRY. New York H.W. Wilson 1959, Pages 165–167.
Fleming, A.M. PIONEERS IN PRINT: ADVENTURES IN COURAGE. Chicago: Reilly & Lee, 1972, Pages 100–113.

MAHALIA JACKSON
(1911-1972)

Five year old Mahalia Jackson was excited. This was the day she was going to audition for the choir at the Baptist Church on Water Street in New Orleans, Louisiana, the town where she was born.

The songs she knew had been passed down from one generation of blacks to the next. The songs were called spirituals.

At the tryout the choir leader called out, "Next!"

Mahalia stepped forward and began to sing. She needed no accompaniment. "I'm so glad/ I'm so glad," she sang.

Everyone smiled at her. "We shall be glad to have the little girl with the big voice in our choir," someone said.

Mahalia's heart was full of happiness. She loved to sing. Now she could sing in the church choir! But her joy soon turned to sorrow. Her mother was sick.

One day, after Mahalia had been playing along the

tracks, she came home later than usual. "Your mother died," a neighbor told her.

The night, after her mother's funeral, Mahalia went to live at the home of her Aunt Duke and her husband, Emanuel Paul. Her other aunts took in four of Mahalia's brother and sisters. Her brother Peter, five years older than she, lived with Aunt Duke too.

She missed her father, a light-skinned man who loaded ships for a living. At night and on Saturdays he had a little shop where he barbered, and he preached Holiness creed on Sundays.

Mahalia often visited her father on Saturdays. She went to his barber shop because her father's new wife did not like Mahalia and did not make her welcome in her home.

When Mahalia was eleven her Aunt Hannah from Chicago visited Aunt Duke and Uncle Emanuel. She wanted Mahalia to go back to Chicago with her.

"No Jim Crow in Chicago," Aunt Hannah said.

Mahalia grew up where Jim Crow ruled. Jim Crow meant that being black made a difference in what you could do and what you could not do. Mahalia couldn't go to the same school with white children; she couldn't go to the circus with whites; she couldn't worship God in white churches; she couldn't be served in white restaurants, and she had to sit in the back when she rode on buses.

It wasn't the Jim Crow laws that made Mahalia decide to go to Illinois with Aunt Hannah. It was the opportunity to become a nurse that intrigued Mahalia.

"There's plenty of work here in Chicago," Aunt Hannah told Mahalia when they arrived in Chicago. "You can do washings. You can straighten peoples' hair."

Mahalia accepted a couch on the drafty sun porch

much more easily than she accepted Aunt Hannah's suggestions for jobs. After all she had come north for an opportunity to better herself.

Chicago made Mahalia homesick. People were cold. Nobody seemed to care how you felt. They were not courteous and polite the way people were in New Orleans.

As she walked from the elevated train each evening after work as a laundress, she looked for a church to join. She wanted a church were she could sing the way she had learned to sing as a child.

Soon she found the right church. It was the Greater Salem Baptist Church. She was asked to try out for the choir.

At the audition Mahalia was nervous. She couldn't read music. She didn't know exactly what people were talking about when they talked about harmony and the structure of chords. She had learned to sing by listening. She had listend to the records of Ma Rainey and Bessie Smith. Blues singers had been the ones who really taught her to sing. She hoped that God would understand that she learned to sing His praises by listening to the sinners and the unsaved.

"Miss Jackson," the choir master said.

Mahalia whispered the first words. She wanted to get the range allowed her by the acoustics of the room:

"Oh, han' me down/han' me down/

Han' me down yo' sil-vah trumpet/ Ga-briel?" she sang.

When she finished the first verse, the choir room was full of people who came from all parts of the church, drawn together by her singing. Her singing had even brought people in from the street.

She was made a soloist.

It wasn't long before Mahalia was also singing in a quintet. Its members were the minister's three sons and another girl, Louise Barry. They called themselves the Johnson Gospel Singers. Soon they were singing all over the South Side and in churches in downstate Illinois.

They did not expect to make any money. These were depression times.

Mahalia's work was washing clothes on a corrugated washboard, and then hanging them out to dry in the penetrating winds blowing off Lake Michigan.

Many times she asked herself, "Am I going to be doomed to a washtub all my life?"

People who heard her sing in the quintet suggested she take singing lessons and become a professional singer.

Louise Barry encouraged her. "I should take lessons too," she said.

So the girls made an appointment with Professor DuBois.

The Professor was a light-skinned man with a flourishing manner and an affectation in his voice.

"Let me hear you," the Professor said handing her a piece of music. The title was, "Standing in the Need of Prayer." Mahalia did not know how to read the music but she knew the song.

Mahalia searched her memory for the words and the melody. As the Professor began playing she began: "It's me, it's me, O Lawd. . ."

The Professor banged the keys in exasperation. "That's the trouble with you blacks from the South," he said. You can't get the South out of you. Now sing it slowly and sadly like this." The Professor proceeded to sing each syllable distinctly.

Mahalia listened. This was not her way of singing. The Professor's way didn't make her feel good. She felt it didn't bring the Lord's message to listeners the way her peoples' music did.

"Louise," Mahalia told her friend, "this is the first singing lessons I ever took and it is also the last!"

Three years after the Professor rejected her singing Mahalia was hired to do a record.

"Twenty-five dollars for just singing "God's Gonna Separate the Wheat from the Tares?" Mahalia asked the man at the recording company.

To her, in 1934, twenty-five dollars for singing a song she had sung so often in church, was a fortune.

When Mahalia was twenty-four she met and married Isaac Hockenhull. He was a gambling man. There marriage was not a happy one.

Then for five years Mahalia traveled with Thomas Dorsey, a composer. She sang his songs her own way. People loved her everywhere she went. But traveling was tiresome. She came back to Chicago to study beauty culture and flower arranging. She opened Mahalia's Beauty Parlor and Mahalia's house of flowers. She was a success in business and bought property.

Then, in 1946, Mahalia Jackson won fame and fortune. When Mahalia made her big record she was thirty-five years old. The true story of the song "Move On Up a Little High" is not quite clear. One story says that one day when Mahalia was warming up her voice, Bess Berman of Apollo Records heard her. Bess liked the way Mahalia sang the song and asked her to record it right then. Mahalia did and one hundred thousand records were sold in a week.

Her carrer was booming. And just when she needed an

accompanist, Mildred Falls came to her. Mildred knew just what Mahalia wanted. She stayed with Mahalia to the end.

As she continued her career, experts agreed that Mahalia had preserved black singing. She had enriched the storehouse of black American song and in so doing she enriched the spiritual lives of thousands.

As her fame spread she was asked to sing in New York at Carnegie Hall. "After Carnegie Hall you can go anywhere," friends told her.

"Will those fancy white folks understand me?" Mahalia asked.

"Maybe gospel will break down the color line," a friend pointed out.

That made Mahalia decide to sing. It was October 4, 1950, when Mahalia saw thousands of white and black people crowded into Carnegie Hall.

She began to sing, "Sometimes I Feel Like a Motherless child." Then she sang "If You Want to Go to Heaven-Shout."

The audience took to holy dancing, clapping their hands, and crying for joy. Mahalia was carried away by the audience reaction and got down on her knees. When she rose she said:

"Now we must remember we're in Carnegie Hall, and if we cut up too much, they might put us out."

In 1952, television gave Mahalia a chance to sing for a new audience. She was invited to sing in France, England, Holland, Belgium and Denmark.

Mahalia was ill at Bordeau and was rushed to the hospital. She went back to Chicago as soon as she could. She had a serious operation at Billings General Hospital.

In 1956 in Denver, Mahalia met the Reverends King and Abernathy. They wanted her to sing in Montgomery to raise money to pay bail, fines, court costs, and lawyers. She agreed.

When Mahalia and Mildred arrived in Montgomery, the Abernathys showed them hospitality and the Reverend Martin Luther King and his wife came over to assure them how welcome they were.

Dr. King was not a rich man. It would take much money to keep the Civil Rights Movement going. Dr. King was a peaceful man. Mahalia felt he would bring equal rights to blacks. She pledged a considerable part of her fortune to support Dr. King's work.

In 1961 she was thrilled to sing "The Star-Spangled Banner" at the inaugural for President John F. Kennedy.

Then she decided to tour Europe again. She decided to visit the Holy Land too.

The visit to the Holy Land was one of the highest points in Mahalia's life. Since she had joined the choir at the age of five she had been singing about Jericho, the Dead Sea, Galilee, and Bethlehem.

Mahalia said: "Why, it's all still the same! I'm seeing it as Jesus did, with my own eyes.

And now here I am about to walk the streets where Jesus walked and to pray in Calvary and to see and touch all the things I've always sung about. This is my homecoming."

Back home in the 1960's she sang her way across the country. In 1963, the centennial of the Emancipation Proclamation, she joined a huge demonstration in Washington, D.C. A crowd of over 250,000 people gathered. She stood before the crowd and sang. Millions were listening on radio and television as she sang the old spiritual which had come out of the way her people felt.

"I Been Bunked and I Been Scorned" she sang.

In 1971 the government asked her to fly to an American outpost in Japan.

Mahalia was not well. She'd been in and out of hospitals for seven years. But she said "yes." This was her last trip she decided.

But when she got back there was another request waiting for her. Would she go to Germany? There was trouble between the black and white troops there.

Mahalia went. She explained to reporters: "I have hopes that my singing will break down some of the hate and fear that divide the white and black people."

She collapsed on stage in Germany. After hospital care there she was brought back to Illinois to Little Company of Mary Hospital in a Chicago suburb.

Mahalia Jackson died January 27, 1972.

*　　*　　*

BIBLIOGRAPHY (Jackson)

Hughes, Langston, and Meltzer, Milton, BLACK MAGIC; A PICTORIAL HISTORY OF THE NEGRO IN AMERICAN ENTERTAINMENT. New York; Crown, 1967

Jackson, Jessie: MAKE A JOYFUL NOISE UNTO THE LORD. Thomas Y. Crowell Co. New York, 1974

MARY HARRIS JONES
(1830-1930)

In the month of May in 1835 Mary Harris, a frail five year old, waved good-bye to her father. She stood close to her mother who was wearing her Sunday dress, clean white apron, and her special shawl in honor of the occasion. Her brothers sat on the fence posts in front of the house.

For generations the Harrises had lived in County Cork, Ireland. Richard Harris, Mary's father, was the first to break away.

"I'm going to America. There is no future here," he told his family one day.

"Richard," Mary's mother had pleaded, "don't go. You'll be herded into the bottom of a dirty boat and treated like an animal. Many have died at sea on their way to America."

"I shall not die," Richard Harris shouted defiantly. "I shall work hard in that wonderful land, America. I'll

save my money and send for all of you when I have enough money to pay your passages."

After that Mary often wondered if her father meant what he said about going to America. Then one day in May he packed his knapsack, put on his best cap with the big bill, and told them he was leaving.

"Pray for me, Mary," he said to his little girl as he placed a new rosary into her hand.

"I will! I will!" cried Mary, wiping away the tears with the back of the hand that held the rosary.

Richard Harris did well in America. Mary always listened with concentrated attention as her mother read the letters he wrote to them. He wrote that he earned a dollar a day with free room and board. He worked on a crew which was digging a canal.

After five years of hard work, Richard Harris sent for his family. Mary was ten years old. Her father had become an American citizen and because of his naturalization papers, the whole family became Americans.

The Harris family settled in Toronto, Canada, where Mary's father and brothers worked on the railroad.

"I want you to get some education, Mary" Richard Harris told Mary. "Me and the boys will take care of you and Mama."

As unusual as it was for those times, Mary did receive a high school education.

"I want to get still more schooling, Papa," Mary told her father. "I might have to make my own living someday."

"Oh, a pretty little colleen like you don't have to worry. Some good man will take care of you," Mr. Harris said as he dropped a kiss on her forehead.

Mary insisted on more education and took up dressmaking at the same time she went to normal school to become a grammar school teacher.

After a year of teaching, Mary gave up the teaching profession and opened a dressmaking shop in Chicago. She chose Chicago for her shop because Chicago was developing into an important trade center.

Mary's dressmaking establishment did not make enough money to support her properly. She went back to teaching. This time she taught in Memphis, Tennessee.

One day in Memphis she met a man named Robert Jones. He was tall and he was stong and he was a skilled workman. His job as an iron molder was to make tools, plowshares and horseshoes out of hot metal. He talked about the National Molders' Union. Jones wanted to help all workers get more money and better working conditions. He spoke to Mary about his dreams of a better life for workers.

Mary married Bob Jones and shared his dream. They had a happy life together. They had four children.

Then, two years before the Civil War ended, an epidemic of yellow-fever hit Memphis. Mary later told about the epidemic. She said: "We were surrounded by death. Across the street ten persons died. All about my house I could hear weeping and cries of delirium. . ."

One after another, the children died; a few days after they were buried Bob Jones died. At the age of thirty-seven Mary Harris Jones was a childless widow.

Mary threw herself into the work of helping others. She volunteered as a nurse, caring for the sick in hospitals and homes.

Mary thought about what she would do now. In this year, 1867, Chicago was the fastest growing city in the United States. Mary decided to go back to Chicago. She found a suitable location for a dressmaking shop near the lake front.

There were many mansions on Lake Shore Drive. There were many poor in Chicago who lived in foulness and misery.

The rich ladies were Mary's customers. Sometimes as Mary sewed on the luxurious fabrics of ball gowns she glanced out her windows and saw the poor, the jobless and the hungry. She was sorry for them.

Mary was doing a good business and thought she would go on being a dressmaker when a cow owned by Mrs. O'Leary kicked over a keresene lantern. The fire that was started by that lantern lasted three days. Among the buildings burned down in this fire was Mary's dressmaking shop.

Everything Mary had was lost in the fire. At the age of forty-one she had to start again without even a place to live. Mary saw that thousands were in the same predicament and immediately helped organize soup kitchens and helped the sick. She met workers of all kinds.

Most of the iron molders remembered her husband. They gave Mary money, shelter and clothes. Because of the iron molders, Mary again became interested in unions. She helped the union with bookkeeping and wrote up the minutes of their meetings. The molders were part of a labor organization called the Knights of Labor. Mary devoted herself to the Knights of Labor making speeches, enrolling new members, and helping strikers. She was one of the unionists who dared work among the coal miners. Many began to call her "Mother Jones" which became a nickname she had for the rest of her life.

Late in 1885 laboring people began asking for an eight hour day. Mass meetings were held on the Lake Michigan shore front. Many workers and poor people came to these rallies.

69

During the eight hour day campaign, Mother Jones was one of its biggest backers. At a rally for shorter working hours Mary stood before the workers. Many recognized her and cheered.She raised her hand for sielnce and spoke in clear, easy-to-hear tones. Mother Jones said:

"It's time the American worker no longer toiled like a Chinese coolie or a slave in the cotton fields before the Civil War. It's time the American worker got a chance to sit in the sun or go fishing."

Once she used women troops at a mine called Drip Mouth, in Pennsylvania. At Drip Mouth the striking miners knew that interference with the scabs (nonunion men) would bring bloodshed. The miners were ready to give up. Mother Jones called a meeting.

Her voice trembling with emotion, Mother Jones faced the men and said: "Quitters! A fine bunch you are! A disgrace to Ireland! (She knew most of the men were Irish immigrants.) I'll get your wives and daughters and sisters to fight your battles!"

Then, after the meeting with the miners, Mother Jones spoke to the women and girls. "Tomorrow at daybreak I want you at the entrance to Drip Mouth. Bring mops, brooms, rolling pins and frying pans. We're going to form an army and chase those scabs and guards right out of the country. Are you with me?"

"Yes!" the women shouted.

The women's army of Arnor formed at dawn. Mother Jones shouted: "Let's go!"

She ran to the head of the procession brandishing a frying pan and calling out: "Follow me! On to Drip Mouth!"

The outnumbered guards looked at the women in

amazement and fled. The women continued to advance. As they neared the entrance of Drip Mouth, they saw a group of men, whom they knew were not union men, leading mules. With whoops and cries of defiance the women ran toward them holding their kitchen tools high above their heads. The mules were wild with fright. They stampeded. The scabs, hit from every side, ran away too.

The union held a victory celebration. Mother Jones made a speech. She told the miners that this was probably the first strike ever won with mops and brooms.

Mother Jones continued her fight for the unions. Then on a warm day in April, 1903, dressed in a long-sleeved dress with lace collar and cuffs she stood in Independence Square in Philadelphia, Pennsylvania. She looked like a sweet, quiet, helpless little grandmother. Her hair, a silvery-gray, was drawn back in a bun and her silver-rimmed glasses shone in the spring sunshine.

This little old lady was well-known to those who saw her because she had given forty years to the cause of trade unionism. During the past forty years she had faced bullets, jail and physical violence. As an organizer for the United Mine Workers, she brought the union to coal miners in Pennsylvania and West Virginia.

On this day in April she was bringing attention to child labor. She directed a long line of marchers out of Independence Square. The marchers wound around and through the business district and stopped in front of City Hall. A big crowd was waiting to see them.

The children marchers were undersized and so thin and pale that a journalist called them "little gray ghosts." Their faces looked like dull masks. Their eyes showed misery. Some walked with the help of crutches;

some had fingers missing. They were dressed in raggy clothes. Most of the children had no shoes. They marched quietly; they didn't speak and they didn't laugh. There was no band to play marching music for them. There were no banners to fly or slogans to shout. Even though most of them were under twelve years old, they looked like wrinkled old men and women.

These were mill children. Since the age of six they had been working in the textile mills where the air was heavy with lint, making breathing difficult. Their work was dangerous. Often hands were mangled in machines.

The demonstration of the "little grey ghosts" caused a sensation in Philadelphia, especially after Mother Jones spoke to the crowd. She brought some of the children onto the wooden platform with her. She held up their little hands for the audience to see. She ended her talk by exclaiming: "Stop sacrificing children upon the altar of profit!"

Child labor laws were not passed immediately, but just as she had been with other labor troubles, Mother Jones was again a pioneer in the struggle.

As Mary Jones grew older, sickness began taking its toll. Still she kept up with developments in the labor movement. In 1923, at the age of ninety-three, she made a speech at the convention of the Farmer-Labor Party.

She wrote her autobiography and then retired to Silver Springs, Maryland, where she died November 30, 1930. She was one hundred years and six months old.

The labor movement paid her homage. She was buried in Illinois. Illinois was the state in which she had spent most of her life working out of the Knights of Labor office in Chicago.

She was carried by special train to Mt. Olive, Illinois, where the United Mine Workers had a cemetery. Her body laid in state for four days at the Mt. Olive Labor Hall. Mary Harris Jones' funeral was attended by over twenty thousand mourners.

(* * *

BIBLIOGRAPHY (Jones)

Bimba, Anthony: THE HISTORY OF THE AMERICAN WORKING CLASS (New York: International Publishers, 1937)

Dulles, Foster Rhea: LABOR IN AMERICA (New York: Thomas Y. Crowell Co., 1949)

Jones, Mrs. Mary: AUTOBIOGRAPHY OF MOTHER JONES, ed. by Mary Field Parton (Chicago: Charles H. Kerr & Co., 1925)

Yellen, Samuel: AMERICAN LABOR STRUGGLES (New York: Harcourt, Brace & Co., 1936)

HARRIET MONROE
1860 - 1936

Eleven-year-old Harriet Monroe sat up in bed. She listened closely. Strange sounds were coming from downstairs.

"Dora! Dora! Wake up!" Harriet whispered to her older sister across the room.

From beneath a heavy quilt came a mumbled voice. "Go back to sleep. It's not time to get up yet."

A flicker of light appeared in a wall mirror across the room. Then another orange streak danced in the mirror.

Sliding out of bed, Harriet raced to the window. She rubbed her eyes and looked out over the Chicago skyline. Quickly Harriet opened the window.

In the distance, bells tolled, mingling with the muffled sound of people's voices. A patch of smoke seemed to cloak the houses and other buildings like a lazy fog.

Fire! The city was on fire!

Harriet turned and ran to her sister's bed. Quickly she

pulled Dora up and almost carried the confused girl to the window.

"Look over there!" Harriet whispered, the fear causing her voice to shake. "There's a fire by the river."

For a moment the two girls stood silently. Hearing a shout from downstairs, Harriet dashed to the bedroom door. She almost ran into her father as she darted into the hallway.

"Father! Have you seen—"

Mr. Monroe shook his head. "I've not time to talk with you, Harriet. Go back into your room."

"But the fire, Father. It looks like it's burning the whole city! Where's mother? Do you think—"

Shoving his daughter back into her room, Mr. Monroe wiped his forehead with his sleeve. "Your mother is with Lucy and Will. You and Dora might go to their room so you'll all be together. Yes, do that. You'll be in no danger here. Now, do as I say, Harriet."

Harriet hurried to get Dora. Minutes later the two girls joined their mother and the other two members of the Monroe family.

"Is it awful?" Dora asked, taking her mother's hand. "Can't they stop the fire?"

"What about Father's office?" murmured Harriet. "The fire looks like it's near—"

Mrs. Monroe pulled her children close to her. "Everything will be all right. We mustn't worry. Your father will take care of things."

It was many days before the extent of the damage caused by the Chicago Fire on October 8, 1871, was actually known. Among the losses in the $187,000,000 disaster were the complete books, records and law offices of Henry Monroe, Harriet's father. But for all the strain placed on the family budget, there was no suggestion of Harriet changing schools. Whatever else would be sacrificed, young Harriet was to receive a quality education.

Until she was sixteen, Harriet attended Chicago schools. Her teachers quickly recognized the young girl's flair for writing.

"Harriet, will you share your composition with the class?" her teachers would say. "It's such a perfect example of clear, crisp writing."

At first Harriet was bashful, somewhat unwilling to recite before her classmates. But gradually she acquired confidence in her own skills. Eagerly she volunteered to share her work and receive comments.

At sixteen, Harriet traveled east to attend the Visitation Convent Boarding School in Georgetown. Quickly the dream to become a poet began to take on definite form.

During the winter of 1888-89, Harriet spent time in New York City. Caught up in the giant city's cultural maze, she visited art galleries, and attended concerts. Opening nights at the theatre offered special thrills. Wanting to share the events with her friends back home, Harriet began sending reviews and articles to the Chicago Tribune. When she returned from the East, she was hired at once by the Tribune as an art critic.

More and more people began to read Harriet Monroe's writing. Not satisfied with merely reviewing, she turned to poetry to share her deeper feelings and emotions. In 1892 she published her first book, "Valeria and Other Poems." The book was a quick success, thrusting Harriet into the realm of professional writers.

The fun of her eastern travels led Harriet into more distant journeys. First it was a cruise to Europe; then came a long visit to the western United States. When she finally returned to Chicago, Harriet had accumulated a tremendous collection of poetry written during her travels. Eager to share her new work, Harriet rented a large hall and mailed out four hundred invitations for two poetry readings.

The readings were a disaster. Harriet stood at a podium on the stage. Before her were rows and rows of empty seats.

"I have been gone too long," Harriet told a friend later. "I was foolish to believe people would remember. A poet must keep producing constantly and be heard from often, if he or she is ever to achieve any lasting attention."

After a few feeble attempts at playwriting, as well as a halfhearted fling with essays, Harriet again returned to her first writing love—poetry. But this time she was determined to cast a true "spotlight" on this art. Galleries, museums, orchestras—all enjoyed rich endowments, even from public tax dollars. Why not poetry?

"It's time poetry enjoyed its proper position in the arts," Harriet told her friends. "And I'm going to see that it does!"

Carefully Harriet made her plans. If one hundred Chicago men would pledge fifty dollars yearly for five years, a new poetry magazine could be published. Hopefully, at the end of five years, the magazine could be self-supporting.

"It can't be done!" one of Harriet's friends told her. "No businessman wants to put his money into poetry."

Harriet's eyes flashed with determination. "We won't know until we try!"

Harriet's campaign to raise funds began in September, 1911. She was fifty years old. Displaying a friendly smile and cheerful manner, Harriet started her visits. No secretary could prevent her from meeting the businessman she wanted to see.

One afternoon Harriet sat in the office of a rich Chicago lawyer. The gentleman had remained unconvinced about the importance of a poetry magazine.

"Have you never read Tennyson?" Harriet asked. "Or Longfellow?"

The lawyer nodded. "Of course, but they are gone now. If you could publish a Longfellow—"

"Who says that we cannot?" Harriet interrupted. "If you have read Tennyson, or Longfellow or any other poet, you have a debt with them. They have given you satisfaction, insight, joy. Perhaps with only a few dollars, you may help give birth to another Longfellow."

The lawyer smiled. "Miss Monroe, I shall sign a pledge. But should you ever stop being a poet, you might also consider becoming a lawyer. I could use a partner like you."

In less than a year, Harriet had raised the funds she needed. Poets received invitations to submit to a new magazine—"Poetry." There would be no limitation on length, subject matter or style. Quality would be the sole standard of selection. Best of all, poets would actually be paid for their accepted work!

The first issue of "Poetry: a Magazine of Verse" rolled off the presses September 23, 1912. Displaying a flying Pegasus on the cover, the pages revealed a variety of inner observations and moods.

"History has been made with the beginning of this new arts magazine," wrote one newspaper editor. "People everywhere owe Harriet Monroe much gratitude for her commendable effort. Poets should cheer her with both pens and voices."

Poets found even a more useful way of displaying their

thanks. Manuscripts flooded Harriet's desk. Vachel Lindsay, John Masefield, Alfred Noyes, Louis Untermeyer, Amy Lowell, Carl Sandburg, Edith Wharton, Ezra Pound, Edward Arlington Robinson—all the great poets of the world submitted their work with the hopes of finding publication in "Poetry: a Magazine of Verse."

One night at the magazine office, Harriet entertained a number of her friends. As the evening wore on, two voices could be heard over the others.

"Rhythm is the basis of any truly great poem," argued a short man, his hair flapping wildly as he spoke. "You must have strong rhythm."

The woman before him simply shook her head. "It is even more important that the word be the exact meaning the poet wishes to express. The entire emotion can be shattered without the right word. A visual image can be lost completely."

Others at the party crowded around. For hours the argument between Harriet and Robert Frost raged, as their supporters in the audience clapped and cheered.

But there was no argument at all about the effect "Poetry: a Magazine of Verse" was having on the country. Circulation climbed rapidly. In offices, schools and homes, Harriet's magazine enjoyed wide readership. Her editorials constantly demanded that poetry maintain its rightful position as "Cinderella of the Arts." Whenever she felt the quality of poetry was slipping, she scolded the poets. With rugged determination she warned against poetry becoming a "fashion" rather a lasting word vehicle with a "loyal and sincere audience."

One morning, as Harriet sat on a rolling train, she noticed a small girl seated nearby. Propped in her lap, the red-haired child held the most recent issue of "Poetry."

"Do you like that magazine?" Harriet asked gently.

The girl looked over and smiled. "It has nice words. I don't know what they all mean, but I like the sound of them. Someday I'll know what all the poems mean."

Harriet nodded. "Perhaps you would like to receive the magazine in the mail?"

"Oh, I would!" the girl exclaimed.

"Then that's just what you will have," Harriet answered, taking a pencil from her purse. "If you give me your name and address, I'll see that you get a copy each time one comes out."

Around the world, the magazine that Harriet Monroe had started became the real "voice" of the professional poet. Cash prizes awarded by "Poetry" provided struggling poets with renewed confidence in their talents. W. H. Auden, James Dickey, William Carlos Williams and Sara Teasdale joined the ranks of those published in the magazine.

In 1936 the international meeting of P.E.N., a professional literary organization, was held in Buenos Aires, Argentina. Although she was seventy-five, Harriet agreed to represent the city of Chicago. Asked to speak at the meeting, she consented willingly.

"Our poets have a grand story to tell, and they are telling it in song and rhythmic words with gusto, power, and beauty," she told the audience.

Two weeks after the speech Harriet Monroe died. People everywhere mourned the passing of one who had brought new life and spirit to the written word.

"As an editor and a poet, Harriet Monroe had few equals," said her friend Carl Sandburg. "It always gave me a special sense of pride to have come from Illinois, the same place from which Harriet had come. As long as poetry lives, Harriet Monroe will be remembered."

*   *   *

BIBLIOGRAPHY (Monroe)

Cahill, Daniel J. HARRIET MONROE. New York: Twayne Publishers, 1973.

Colum, Mary. LIFE AND THE DREAM. New York: Doubleday and Company, 1947.

Gregory, Horace and Marya Zaturenska. A HISTORY OF AMERICAN POETRY: 1900-1940. New York: Harcourt, Brace and Company, 1942.

Monroe, Harriet. A POET'S LIFE. SEVENTY YEARS IN A CHANGING WORLD. New York: The Macmillan Company, 1938.

Monroe, Harriet and Alice Corbin Henderson (editors). THE NEW POETRY, AN ANTHOLOGY OF TWENTIETH CENTURY VERSE IN ENGLISH. New York: The Macmillan Company, 1923.

Smith, Alson. CHICAGO'S LEFT BANK. Chicago: Henry Regnery Company, 1953.

ARCHANGE OUILMETTE
(1764-1840)

One day three little Potawatomi girls were playing in
the forest. It was late fall, after the harvest, and the
people were beginning to separate into smaller groups
and move to temporary hunting camps spread throughout the lush forests of Illinois. They needed to be near
wild game.

"We will not see you until spring, Archange," one of
the black-eyed girls said turning toward the tallest one.

"Yes, that is true," replied Archange. "Perhaps my
father will not stay in our wigwam until then. He
trades."

"The white man has strange ways," nodded the third.
Then she cocked her head to one side and asked, "Do you
love a white father?"

Archange, who was always being reminded that even
though her mother was Potawatomi, her father was
French, felt compassion for both the Indians and the
whites.

"You look Potawatomi," her mother assured her often
as she stroked Archange's thick black hair with the blue

sheen of lights running through it. "But your father's blood has refined your features to the delicateness of the rosebud."

Archange lived a busy life in her growing years. She accepted the Potawatomi ways, but enjoyed speaking French to her father and of hearing of life far across the waters. She often helped her father trade corn when there was an overabundance. French traders came to know her. Beans, squash, pumpkins and melons were also traded. Sometimes there was tobacco to trade. Sometimes Archange traded wild rice, berries, nuts and roots.

Although Potawatomi braves asked for her hand, Archange always shook her head "no."

And then one autumn, when the land yielded its glorious abundance, a tall Frenchman came to the shore in a merchandise-ladened canoe. Archange looked deep into the Frenchman's eyes and a bond of love between them began. It was a bond that was to last a lifetime.

In 1796, the daughter of Francois Chevallier and a Potawatomi woman was married to Antoine Ouilmette. It was a wedding befitting the bride.

"I want to be married in the woods with the good earth at my feet, the trees as our witnesses, and the Great Spirit looking down at us from a clear blue sky," it is reported Archange said.

It was as she wished. They were married in the woods of Grosse Point, near several Potawatomi villages. Hundreds of guests were in attendance. It was an Indian-Christian ceremony. A priest was in attendance.

The couple went back to Antoine's cabin. He had arrived in the little Indian settlement called Checaugau in July, 1790. This huddle of huts and teepees lay along the banks of the river by the same name. Apparently it attracted him as a place to settle for the trade in furs with the Indian trappers, which, as a representative of the American Fur Company, was the business which brought him through the forests and streams from his native home at Lahndrayh, near Montreal.

This spot was so much a part of the Ouilmette headquarters that it has set up a good claim for being "the first permanent white settlement" of the community which later became Fort Dearborn and still later the mighty cross-roads of America, Chicago.

Archange bore eight children, four sons and four daughters.

In August, 1812, Archange and her family were responsible for saving two lives during the old Fort Dearborn massacre by the Potawatomis.

Fort Dearborn had been built in 1803 and named after General Henry Dearborn. When the War of 1812 began, the fort was commanded by Captain Nathan Heald. Heald was ordered to leave the fort and move his troops and the settlers to the safer Detroit area. Although his troops on the fort urged their commander not to leave the fort because of the danger of an Indian attack, Heald decided to obey orders and on August 15, 1812, marched out of the fort with 67 soldiers and 30 settlers. But when the party had reached what is now 18th Street near Lake Michigan, a band of 500 Potawatomis attacked the small force, and killed half the group, returning the next day to burn Fort Dearborn.

The next day another group of Potawatomis arrived at the site. They were angry because they had missed the massacre and the plunder, they were determined to take revenge on the few survivors, including a prominent officer's wife, Mrs. Helm.

Black Partridge, the Potawatomi chief, who had saved Mrs. Helm's life during the first attack, told her to dress as a French woman, and took her to the Ouilmette's house.   88

"Will you help save this white woman who has done no harm to our people?" asked the chief.

Archange circled the confines of the small cabin room looking for a possible hiding place. Archange's sister rocked unconcernedly on a sturdy oak rocker, the garment on which she was stitching absorbing all her attention.

"Good," said Archange.

"Get over to the bed," she ordered Mrs. Helm.

The wide-eyed panic-stricken Mrs. Helm obeyed.

"Now," said Archange, "get under the feather bed."

"But . . . but . ." protested Mrs. Helm, "the heat is intense today. It is so hot in this room."

"The heat will not kill you, but the Potawatomi will," replied Archange.

When Mrs. Helm was under the feather bed, Archange ordered her sister to continue the sewing as she sat on the bed.

When the Indians entered the house, she sat calmly working on her sewing, until the war party left.

Archange smiled and said a silent prayer of thanks.

Then, just as the Indians left, a noncommissioned officer named Griffin, who had escaped the massacre climbed into the house through a window.

Archange offered him a cool drink and expressed a thankfulness that he was still alive. "My people," she sighed, "they feel such grievances toward the white man. It is so wrong for them to kill. But I love them, too. They are my people.

Take off your uniform" Archange commanded.

The officer obeyed without a word. He trusted this woman. He knew her reputation as being kind, compassionate and trustworthy.

Archange opened a crude chest at the foot of the bed.

She took out a deerskin suit, with belt, moccasins and pipe, like those used by French traders.

"Now you may walk out the door in safety," Archange said.

The officer knelt before her and kissed her hands. The gratefulness in his heart overwhelmed all speech.

The Ouilmette family stayed on in the cabin after all other white settlers had fled. They were very likely the only white settlers in Chicago for the next four years.

In 1814, when the Fort was rebuilt, they sold crops to the new commander, Captain Bradley. Archange and her husband were thrifty and ambitious. They built up a herd of oxen, horses and cattle, operated a small store, continued to trade with the Indians, and sold wool from their sheep to make yarn for stockings for the soldiers.

According to a Chicago tax roll dated July 25, 1825, Antoine paid $4.00 in taxes on property valued at $400.00, and the following year listed as a voter in the election on August 7, casting his vote for John Quincy Adams for president.

Shortly after voting for President Adams, Antoine and Archange moved north and built a cabin overlooking the lake, just north of Lake Avenue. White settlers were now beginning to move into northern Illinois, and by the summer of 1827, the Indians of the region were restless and angry, resenting the movement of the whites into their lands.

On July 29, 1829, the Treaty of Prairie du Chien was concluded, giving the United States title to huge areas of land from Lake Michigan west to the Rock River. Signing the document were thirty Indian braves and five squaws, representing the Chippewas, Ottawas and Potawatomis.

Most important, the treaty also created the original

Ouilmette Reservation. Article Four provided for a grant of land to Archange Ouilmette, in recognition of the help she had given in persuading the Indians to sign the Treaty.

These two sections consisted of about 300 acres which fell within the present boundaries of Evanston, Illinois.

In April, 1833, at the pleadings of Archange, Antoine sent a petition for Chicago's first Catholic church to the Bishop of the Missouri diocese in St. Louis. Staunch Catholics, Archange and her husband, urged the bishop that a "priest should be sent there before other sects obtain the upper hand, which very likely they will try to do." The bishop acted very quickly, granting the request for what was to be Mary's Church on April 17, only a day after the petition was received.

Antoine and Archange lived on the Ouilmette Reservation until 1838.

Both in their late seventies, the Ouilmette's decided to move west with the Potawatomis across the Mississippi. In November, 1840, Archange died at Council Bluffs, Iowa, and Antoine followed her in December, 1841.

*　　*　　*

BIBLIOGRAPHY (OUILMETTE)

"Wilmette: A History" by George D. Bushnell (1976)
"Evanston's Yesterdays" by Clyde D. Foster (1956)
"Illinois Guide and Gazetteer" Rand McNally & Co.
"Indian Treaties 1778–1883" Interland Publishing Inc.
"American Indians" Compiled by Edward E. Hill 1981
"Journal of the Illinois State Historical Society" Published by The Illinois State Historical Society at Springfield Illinois . . 1944

BERTHA HONORE PALMER
(1849-1918)

Bertha Honoré was thirteen when her mother pointed out that she was being admired by one of her father's guests, Mr. Potter Palmer. Bertha moved with grace against the background of ancestral French furniture, in her father's Chicago home. Her dark hair fell in long strands over her shoulders and was looped behind her ears with tiny bows.

She was flattered that Potter Palmer, Chicago's richest bachelor, was charmed by her looks and manners. She saw him watching her. He was thirty-six years old, owned the most talked of store in the country, and made millions in real estate.

Bertha smiled and moved a little closer to Mr. Palmer's group. Mr. Palmer was talking about John Wilkes Booth who was playing Richard III at the McVickers Theater. Mr. Booth was the hit of the year. It was 1862.

Bertha, without being too obvious, took careful notice of Mr. Palmer. She liked him. He was a reserved man, stockily built, with dark brown hair, and keen blue eyes. She enjoyed the way his eyes twinkled when he thought something was funny.

Bertha was quick to sense that her parents liked Mr. Palmer too. Her parents were descendents from distinguished Southern families. They had moved from Louisville to Chicago in 1855. Chicago was growing up and her father bought and subdivided and built and improved property.

Bertha, her sister and her four brothers liked growing up in the city. And, after that first meeting between Bertha and Mr. Palmer, whenever Mrs. Honoré went shopping, Bertha accompanied her mother to Mr. Palmer's store.

Everyone noticed that when Bertha Honoré came to the Palmer store, Mr. Palmer dropped whatever he was doing to pull out bolts of silks and to hunt for just the right gloves.

The battles of the Civil War were far from Chicago, but Bertha was always aware of it. The Honoré home was always open to every good cause for the war effort.

No sooner had Chicago celebrated the end of the war than news of the assassination of Lincoln stunned the city. Bertha saw the funeral train pass through Chicago on its way to Springfield. A slow processional wound its way to the courthouse while thousands of people passed in double file past the bier.

It was that fall that Bertha entered the Convent of the Visitation in Georgetown. Before she left, she went to see Potter Palmer. She paid a proper visit to bid him "good-bye" for he was going to Europe for his health.

"I'm waiting for you to grow up, Bertha," Mr. Palmer

said seriously. "When you are a woman, I'm going to ask you to marry me."

In the days to come, Bertha wondered if he was serious. She decided he was.

On a June day in 1867 she was graduated from the Convent of the Visitation. She was one of six students to receive highest honors. In fact she felt embarrassed at the list of honors she was given. She was honored for her grades in history, ancient and modern geography, chemistry, meteorology, astronomy and botony, logic and intellectual philosophy, rhetoric, literature and composition, algebra and geometry, manual work and domestic economy. She also took top honors in piano, harp, and vocal music.

The nuns remembered her for her intelligence and tact.

That fall Bertha made her debut in the new Honore' home on Michigan Avenue. She was as usual surrounded by the heirlooms of her French ancestors. Now Potter Palmer made no secret of the fact that he wanted to marry her.

"Bertha," her mother said one day shortly after the debut, "the uniformed messengers with flowers for you from Mr. Palmer have been coming in a steady procession. Are you going to marry him?"

"I haven't quite made up my mind," Bertha smiled. "I'm having such a good time with so many of the eligible young men of Chicago."

But in 1870 when the Palmer House (a fine hotel) was finished and Bertha was twenty-one, she said "yes" to Potter Palmer. His wedding gift to her was the $3,500,000 Palmer House.

The Potter Palmers were not established in their country home on the outskirts of Chicago very long when one October night a catastrophe happened.

It was at the time of Bertha's first separation from her husband who was in New York attending the funeral of one of his sisters. Bertha stood at the window watching the oak leaves twirl and swirl by the autumn wind when an eerie yellowish glow hanging over the city caught her eye. Then she saw shafts of flame shoot across the skyline. Her hand went to her throat in fear.

"It looks like the whole city is on fire!" she gasped aloud.

As she watched with frightened fascination, blazes appeared here and there. They illuminated the scene and Bertha could see the frantic population of the city. The streets were jammed with fleeing families. They ran in all directions. The noise was unearthly. There were explosions as oils and paints were touched off. Bertha realized that the Palmer and Honoré fortunes were going up in flames.

"Chicago shall rise again," Bertha whispered as the tears streamed down her face.

She took in as many of the homeless as she could accommodate.

All the days that followed were busy days for Bertha. She took the greatest interest in her husband's reconstruction efforts. She was side by side with her husband and her father as they worked to make Chicago a habitable city again and a commercial center of the first importance.

"I have more than I bargained for, Bertha," Mr. Palmer said one night. "I not only have a beautiful wife and a stimulating companion, but I have a helpmate as well."

"I love Illinois, Potter," she said, "and Chicago in particular. I want to help you to help Chicago."

She proved what she said was true because she became more and more interested in public work. She opened her home for the Chicago Woman's Club as a money raising feat. Bertha was an enthusiastic and always active member of the Woman's Club. She was also actively interested in the Woman's Temperance Union. She worked for Jane Addams of Hull House. She held meetings for factory girls at her home and studied the conditions under which they lived and worked.

She had two sons, Potter and Honoré whom both she and Mr. Palmer adored. Bertha spent much of her time with her boys as they were growing up. Mr. Palmer told a friend that one of his pleasures was watching Bertha romp with the boys.

One day Potter Palmer came home and taking Bertha by the hand and dropping a kiss on her nose he said: "I'm going to build a new house in the middle of some reclaimed land. The house will face the lake and it will be looking toward Lincoln Park.

"I'll help with the plans, Potter!" Bertha exclaimed, her dark eyes shining.

For the next three years the two of them worked on their castle. When it was finished the castle was described as early English, battlemented style. Some said it was merely an adaptation of Gothic. Its tower, with a spiral staircase, rose eight feet high. At first Mr. Palmer thought it might cost as much as ninety thousand to build the castle. When it was finished it cost more than a million dollars. Mr. Palmer would never tell how much more.

Then came the excitement of the World's Columbian Exposition. It was to be held in Chicago. Bertha Palmer became the President of the National Board of Lady Managers of the Columbian Exposition. The appointment fired Bertha with excitement and ambition.

"Oh, Potter!" she exclaimed. "If I just can get foreign rulers to get women's exhibits for the Fair. I plan to bring together women of all nations. I am looking at the role of women for this event in large terms."

"You have a bold idea," Potter kissed his wife's cheek, "but knowing you, even the building will be designed by a woman architect!"

Bertha smiled and her dark eyes shone. This Columbian Exposition was even a greater challenge than the Charity Balls she gave every season.

Bertha took off for an extended tour in Europe. She contacted the heads of state either by letter or by personal contact. By the time she stepped off the Normannia in July, 1891, forty-one countries were ready to exhibit in the Woman's Building.

"But the real triumph," she told Potter, "will be the building itself!"

There was a contest for sketches of a Woman's Building. Sketches were to be submitted only by women. Sophia G. Hayden, a twenty-one year old graduate of the Massachusetts School of Technology, won. She was the first woman to design an important public building in the United States. Bertha liked her plans, but did request that she add a roof garden.

Next to the Women's Building there was to be a Children's Building. In December, 1892, Bertha threw open her home for the Columbian Bazaar of all Nations to raise money for the Children's Building at the Fair. Thirty five thousand dollars (a great sum of money at this time) was raised. Mothers and educators all over the country worked for this building too and every child who subscribed got a printed certificate stamped with a gold seal.

Bertha Palmer looked forward to the dedication ceremonies of the Exposition. It was October 1892 and the Windy City was becoming the Dream City of the nation.

Bertha wore a gown of yellow satin and velvet. Ropes of pearls hung from her throat. Her dark hair was crowned with a diamond tiara. She led the procession of patronesses as the long parade marched to the tune of the "Coronation March." The music was played by Sousa's band.

As Bertha walked around the Women's Building, a glow of pleasure filled her. The building was two stories high and had land and water entrances. Its Hall of Honor was seventy feet high and was inscribed in gold with the names of women great in art, music, in science, in stagecraft, and in letters. She thought how lucky she was to have Mary Cassatt do one of her murals. Twenty five panels in the building were the work of American women and Bertha heard often that these murals were the most discussed ones at the Fair. She glowed with pleasure at this compliment.

"You were magnificent," Potter Palmer told his wife as they breakfasted in the sunny breakfast room. "With that golden nail you drove into the Women's Building and with the words you said, you honored all the women of the world."

After the Exposition Bertha and her husband continued to add to their art collection. Potter Palmer added a gallery to their mansion and many societies from America and from abroad came to view the Palmer paintings. The paintings covered three periods. . .the Romantic, the Barbizon and the Impressionist.

Bertha was looked on as a true pace setter in art by authorities of the day. "She had an open mind and an alert eye for new trends and her interest in art was

genuine," one authority was quoted as saying.

After Bertha Palmer became widowed she developed land in Sarasota, Florida and thanks to her influence Sarasota pushed ahead as a popular resort area.

But until the end, her fixed ambition to push Chicago ahead financially and culturally dictated her actions for the better part of her lifetime. She was a wealthy woman who spent money with zeal for the public welfare.

Bertha Palmer died May 5, 1918. She was sixty-nine years old.

*   *   *

BIBLIOGRAPHY (Palmer)

Bancroft, Hubert Howe: THE BOOK OF THE FAIR COLUMBIAN EDITION. Chicago: The Bancroft Company 1893

Bowen, Louise de Koven: GROWING UP WITH A CITY. New York: The Macmillan Company 1926

Dedmon, Emmett: FABULOUS CHICAGO. New York: Random House, 1953

James, Henry: THE AMERICAN SCENE. New York Haper & Brothers, 1897

Ross, Ishbel: SILHOUETTE IN DIAMONDS. New York: Harper & Brothers, Publishers, 1960

LUCY FITCH PERKINS
1865-1937

Lucy was sent to her room again. She was a fighter. A prima donna's urge to take center stage was the reason for Lucy fighting her own fights and also those of everyone she loved.

"I don't care," she shouted over her shoulder as she defiantly climbed the stairs to her room.

There was always pencil and paper in her room, although in the frugal Fitch household, paper was not always easy to come by.

Hour after hour she lay on the floor close under the sloping ceiling of her little dormer window, and drew and drew until the anger had ebbed away and she had restored herself to happiness.

She was only twelve years old in 1877 but even at this tender age her active imagination and unusual preoccupation with such things as the shifting of the patches of sunlight on the parlor floor, the finding of treasured

color and shapes in her mother's button box, the sensation of dogs barking through the cold clarity of a winter night, stirred reactions within her.

Lucy was the second in a family of five sisters. Her father, a scholar and gifted teacher, was forced by the Civil War and the subsequent hard times, as well as the needs of his family, to go into the lumber business in the frontier forests of Indiana. Her mother was a teacher, and between the two of them, managed to make a life for their girls in the forest clearing, and in small towns of Michigan and Massachusetts, exemplifying the best and sturdiest of America before the machine age. Although the family had little money, they thought themselves rich in the things that mattered.

Lucy grew up in a scholarly world despite the family's simple standard of living. She reaped the benefits of her father's classical education through endless stories, as well as the great books read to them daily.

She sang regularly in church. The happy high points of her childhood were circus parades, sleigh rides and candy pulls.

After high school the family pooled their resources and Lucy was sent to the art school at the Museum of Fine Arts in Boston, and she studied there for three years.

On the morning of June first of her last week in school, she was working over a difficult pose in life class when a latecomer brought her a letter, saying that a young man had asked her to deliver it, and he was waiting now at the door of the museum for an answer. Lucy, irritated by her inability to get the planes correctly, and by the fact that her teacher had just told her that the whole thing was too vague, glared angrily at the letter. She saw that it was dated in the previous September and was from her Uncle Edwin Bennett of Chicago, who wanted to introduce her to his wife's young cousin Dwight Heald Perkins, a student of architecture at the Massachusetts Institute of Technology. Dwight was "a fine young man away from home for the first time," and Uncle Ed suggested that Lucy might like to be like a Boston mother to him.

Lucy slammed down her paint brushes. Mothering a young man was the last thing she wanted at this time. With her eyeshade askew and her paint-daubed apron bunched around her waist, she ran down the stairs to get rid of Dwight Heald Perkins.

A slender young man stood with his back to her near the entrance, looking absorbedly at some architectural renderings of the Trinity Place Church that were hung in the corridor. Even though he must have heard her coming he did not turn around.

"Mr. Perkins," Lucy announced.

He turned and looked down at her. His deep-set hazel eyes were gentle but impersonal.

"Miss Fitch," he replied.

"I see it has taken you nearly a year to deliver my uncle's message," she said.

"Yes. I didn't want to go home and tell him I hadn't met you. He wouldn't understand how hard they keep me on the buzz at Tech."

The artist feeling in her, that had always remained strong and true, had reacted accurately and innately to something in Dwight, although in her conscious thinking she was unable to recognize what had happened.

The story of Lucy after she was married was necessarily the story of her husband and of his work; of her children and of the community in which the family lived, for she was an ardent homemaker and good neighbor. The part that belonged to her alone concerned her work.

At the time of Dwight and Lucy's wedding in 1891, Queen Victoria was alive and her influence was strong. Lucy accepted the Victorian code which professed a wife's economic dependence.

Furthermore, Dwight Perkins did not believe that Lucy should renounce her talents. As a wedding present to her, he designed a beautiful studio room in the house he had built.

The time came when Lucy had to remember her career. Prosperity collapsed when Chicago almost disintegrated in the panic and depression of the early eighteen-nineties. The city had overexpanded and overbuilt to accomplish its great World's Columbian Exposition, and when it was over, business declined sharply.

Dwight was overworried and underworked and became ill. Their home was mortgaged and payments had to be met.

Lucy promptly filled the extra bedrooms in the house with boarders. Then she went to the Chicago office of the Prang Company. She asked to do any job of lettering or illustrating that they might have. She took home a sheaf of work and from that day on was never without paid work.

For the next ten years she taught, lectured, edited, published, illustrated, made mural decorations to enliven schoolrooms, and made an enthusiastic contribution to the foundation of modern education. The more she was recognized, the more it seemed natural to continue her efforts. Dating from 1904, Dwight was recognized as one of the three or four men in the country who were ushering in the magnificent school buildings of the modern era. His success made it unnecessary for Lucy to work, but by that time she could not abandon her own goals and achievements.

It was not until 1912 when "The Dutch Twins" was published that her major work as a maker of books for children began. The idea for the "Dutch Twins" came almost by accident. She had been drawing delightful little Dutch characters one afternoon while she told stories about them to her four year old son. As she worked and he watched, the characters of Kit and Kat and their Dutch house sprang into being, the drawings of them covering the porch floor by the time the little boy was taken away to be fed his supper.

A publishing friend, Mr. Edwin O. Grover, was her dinner guest that evening. He arrived early and in offering to help put the porch in order, he picked up the drawings from the floor.

"You have a book here," he told Lucy excitedly.

Together they sat down and sorted out the beginnings of the story. Lucy saw that the eye of the experienced publisher had been quicker than her own. She acknowledged that she did have a good marketable idea and the next day she retired to her third floor studio to mold the idea into form.

During the week, her business took her into the offices of four firms publishing school and trade books for children. Immediately, she found herself in a most unusual position. She was standing off publishers competing for a book not yet written, by an author who had not written any books.

She was propelled into a twenty-five year writing assignment. Her simple and true little stories were translated into European languages and into Japanese.

To account for the popularity of the Twin series of stories, Lucy Perkins sometimes suggested that the most innate longing of the human soul is not to be lonely. By showing her characters as twins, always together and

always sharing, she had given her young readers a way of meeting the need for a perfect companion.

The second need of the human soul is to laugh. The Twin stories gave plenty of opportunity for that.

Lucy Perkins' work, begun in the late eighteen-eighties, reached its highest point of productivity some fifty years later, when in January, 1935, the two millionth copy of one of her books for children came off the press.

Early in the New Year, word came from Geneva, Switzerland that the publishers had been asked to place all the books by Lucy Fitch Perkins in the League of Nations Library, recognizing their valuable contribution to international friendship.

When Lucy learned about this honor, she knew she had touched her goal.

*　　　*　　　*

Books by Lucy Fitch Perkins. . . . .
THE AMERICAN TWINS, THE INDIAN TWINS, THE SPARTAN TWINS, THE SWISS TWINS, THE ESKIMO TWINS, THE CAVE TWINS, THE PIONEER TWINS, THE JAPANESE TWINS, THE DUTCH TWINS, THE SCOTCH TWINS, THE SPANISH TWINS.

BIBLIOGRAPHY (PERKINS)

"Eve Among the Puritans" by Eleanor Ellis Perkins Houghton Mifflin Co. 1956.
"Contemporary Illustrators"
"The Twins are Back" Walker and Company
"Book of Junior Authors" Kunitz

MYRTLE NORTON WALGREEN
1879 - 1971

Myrtle Norton's eyes widened in surprise as she opened the farmhouse door. On the front porch stood seven strong sturdy men.

"We're here to do the thrashing, Miss," one of the men said. "Is your Mama home?"

Nine-year-old Myrtle shook her head. "She's gone today. Some folks north of here ordered some pin oaks. Mama went to deliver them."

Rubbing his chin, the man spoke again. "Well, we have to get the work done today or we can't do it at all. We'll be heading out to the fields now. Hope you can be seeing about a meal when we get done."

Before she could answer, the men were gone. For a moment Myrtle stood silently. Then suddenly the words ran through her mind again. "Hope you can be seeing about a meal when we get done." The men were there to thrash the wheat on the Norton's 160 acre farm near

Normal, Illinois. When they finished, they would be expecting a good hot dinner. Quickly Myrtle raced to the kitchen and slipped into her blue calico apron.

"Let's see," she said aloud, "they'll want meat, potatoes, vegetables—"

Myrtle was used to being "on her own." Her father had died when Myrtle was only seven and her brother Paul was nine. Lydia Ellen Norton, Myrtle's mother, had no desire to be known as "a poor and helpless widow woman." Quickly she turned her love for plants and flowers into a money-making business. To central Illinois farmers and townspeople, Lydia Norton sold a wide variety of nursery stock.

But their mother's business trips often left Myrtle and Paul home alone. Sometimes there was a housekeeper to care for them, other times they looked after themselves. Daily duties were shared. The two children milked the cows, then cleaned the barn and house. But Myrtle was in charge of the kitchen.

"Um-m. . ." Myrtle inhaled the rich smell of the beef stew she stirred. Minutes later she set a pan of string beans and carrots on the stove to boil. "Now, what for dessert?" she wondered aloud. "I know—lemon custard!"

By the time the men returned from thrashing, a fine table was set before them. The tired and hungry workers ate eagerly, causing Myrtle to smile at the success of her efforts.

Soon it was time for dessert. Myrtle served each of the men a hearty helping of lemon custard.

"Ug-h!" one of the men sputtered as he took a spoonful of custard.

"Get me some more water!" shouted another, dropping his spoon back on his plate. Myrtle took a quick taste of the dessert, then gasped. It was awful!

"Miss, what's in this mixture of yours? Poison?"

Myrtle's face reddened at the question of one of the men. She wanted to cry.

Without warning, the man at the far end of the table arose. He lifted his water glass into the air. "I don't know about everybody else, but I'm so filled up, I don't believe I could eat any dessert if I wanted to. Here's a toast to our fine hostess."

Blushing, Myrtle stood silently as the other men hoisted their water glasses. "Hooray!" they all cheered. "Hooray!"

Myrtle felt better after the men had gone. She was happy and relieved when her mother got home. Without wasting a word, the excited girl shared the story of the disasterous dessert.

"Oh, dear, I should have told you!" Mrs. Norton exclaimed. "I keep a little bottle of machine oil on the top shelf. I didn't have anything else to put it in, so I just put it in an empty lemon extract bottle."

Myrtle's face paled. "I-I put machine oil in the custard? Oh, Mama, I'm so ashamed—"

Mrs. Norton drew her daughter to her. "You needn't be, dear. A little machine oil won't hurt those men. I'm just proud of the way you took charge of everything. Most girls would have been too confused to know what to do. You did just fine."

Myrtle felt good inside. After hugging her mother, she pulled away. "I'm going to throw out the rest of the custard!"

"I'll help you!" her mother laughed.

Life at school for Myrtle was as busy as life at home. By the time she reached high school, she had discovered a talent for speechwork. She enjoyed writing declamations and entering contests.

Not long after her high school graduation, Myrtle found her mother making plans to move the family to Chicago. Paul had been working in a drug store and wanted to continue his studies. He planned to enroll at the Chicago College of Pharmacy.

Finding an apartment in the south side of Chicago, the three Nortons settled in. The apartment was large enough for them to feed boarders in the sunny dining room. Once more, Myrtle took on a busy schedule in the kitchen preparing meals.

But Myrtle was not satisfied with just cooking duties—she wanted something more, something that would offer her challenge and independence. She enrolled at Hyde Park High School, signing up for courses which would prepare her for teaching. The school was three miles from the apartment, yet Myrtle chose to walk both ways.

One evening a friend came to dinner. He kept telling Myrtle she should study shorthand and stenography. Finally, Myrtle demanded to know why he was so interested in her future.

The man smiled. "Well, I want to marry my secretary, but I can't do it until I find somebody good to take her place!"

"Why didn't you say so in the first place?" Myrtle laughed. "I like the idea and you could have saved yourself a lot of words!"

Myrtle enrolled at Gregg Secretarial School. Students could proceed as fast as they could, and Myrtle discovered a sense of rhythm that allowed her to type and write with super speed.

Each morning Myrtle was up at five, practicing at the typewriter. In the evening Paul read the newspaper aloud and she typed out each story. She was determined to get the secretarial job. In six weeks she had finished the school program. No one had ever completed the program that fast. The next day she went to work as a secretary.

"You sure speeded up my marriage plans!" her new boss laughed. "I'm grateful!"

While Myrtle busied herself at her new job, Paul continued his pharmacy studies. He worked at a drugstore to help pay for his courses. One night he came home excited.

"There's a special excursion coming up," Paul told Myrtle. "All the druggists in Chicago will be showing off the products from their stores. It should be fun. Will you help show off the products from the store where I work?"

Myrtle agreed, somewhat hesitantly. She was not sure what she had to do. She soon found out.

On a hot June day in 1900 Paul helped Myrtle down the stairs of the apartment house. She staggered a bit, weighed under by over-size jewelry, wide pennants, heavy belts, a long sash and a flopping hat.

"I feel like a walking Christmas tree!" Myrtle exclaimed. "Does your drugstore really sell all these things?"

Paul laughed. "And much more," he answered.

Carefully Myrtle moved around the people at the excursion. Suddenly she bumped into a tall, handsome stranger.

"Oh, I'm so sorry!" Myrtle moaned.

"That's quite a store you're advertising!" the man chuckled. "May I introduce myself? I'm Charles Walgreen."

From the moment they met, Myrtle liked Charles Walgreen. His eyes sparkled, his laugh came quickly, and he made lively conversation. Much of the talk centered around his future plans.

"I hope to own my own drugstore someday," he told Myrtle. "I want to be my own boss."

Myrtle shared Charles' desire for independence. When he proposed, they agreed their marriage was to be "a real partnership."

"We'll be a team," promised Charles.

Charles found a drugstore he wanted to buy. His down payment was small, but his enthusiasm was great. As soon as he took over, he began opening the store at seven thirty in the morning, and did not close up until eleven at night.

While Charles devoted himself to the store, Myrtle searched for an apartment and furniture. The newlyweds could only afford twenty-five dollars a month rent, but Myrtle finally found a place.

"It's perfect!" Charles exclaimed. "This team is sure to work!"

Charles worked hard at his store, and soon he owned it. Before long he was buying another.

After supper one night, Charles pushed his chair away from the table. "Another delicious meal, dear. I could eat your food all day."

An idea clicked in Myrtle's mind—why couldn't Charles' drugstores offer food for hungry customers?

The idea was tried—and proved a quick success. Each morning Myrtle arose at five and bought fresh chickens down the street. Her ice box was too small to keep the chickens overnight. By seven-thirty, the meat was cooking. Myrtle cut the chicken, using meat slices for sandwiches and the wings and back for chicken salad.

Pies were Myrtle's specialty. She was delighted when Charles told her customers were willing to pay eighty cents for each pie she baked.

In 1904 Myrtle took a vacation—to have a baby. A boy was born—and promptly named Paul. Before he was a year old, the baby became sick. For weeks Myrtle and Charles stayed by their baby's bedside.

But it was hopeless. One night, as Myrtle held her little Paul lovingly, he died.

"We will have another child," Charles comforted his wife. Myrtle nodded, easing her husband's grief, but still feeling the sorrow only a mother knows.

Charles' prediction came true. Two years later, Charles Rudolph was born. In 1910, the proud parents welcomed baby Ruth.

As the Walgreen family grew, so did the Walgreen business. Before long, Charles was selling stock in his drugstore business and allowing men to open Walgreen Drugstores in their own hometowns. "It's hard to explain," he laughed. "These fellows are all smarter than I am, yet they're working for me."

Myrtle constantly offered her opinions about the business, suggesting new products the stores could carry. Her ideas seldom failed.

As their family and business grew, Myrtle and Charles shared a dream. They wanted to buy a farm so they could spend time in the country. In 1929, their dream came true. They purchased two hundred and fifty acres of rolling land outside Dixon along the Rock River. The estate, which had been called"Hazelwood," was covered with weeds and wild bushes. Dead limbs hung sadly from dying trees. Much work was needed.

Quickly Myrtle swung into action. An empty old barn became a lovely new home. A log playhouse, a horse stable, chicken coops—all were built on Hazelwood's acres. Birdhouses were erected, offering shelter to the vast number of blue martins in the area. Myrtle's childhood knowledge of flowers and plants proved valuable as the family transformed Hazelwood into a paradise of colorful blossoms and blooms.

"It's so beautiful," Myrtle told Charles. "We shouldn't keep it all to ourselves."

So it was that Hazelwood began to attract visitors, first in small groups, then in big numbers. Myrtle delighted in the enjoyment people felt in touring the grounds.

In 1939, Charles died of cancer. Myrtle felt alone and sad. Yet she knew she had to go on.

Money posed no problem. The Walgreen drug business was flourishing. Myrtle was a rich woman, rich enough to enjoy the pleasures of wealth in her remaining years.

But Myrtle Walgreen was a "doer." She had no desire simply to exist—she wanted to live, and live with purpose.

The "Beautification of Home Grounds" Program became Myrtle's prime interest. A special 4-H project, youth members of the national organization were rewarded for improving the looks and conveniences of their farm homes.

The Red Cross captured Myrtle's time and energy too. Whether it be knitting clothing or packing canned goods, Myrtle gained satisfaction by contributing her efforts. During World War II, she received a special award for donating two thousand volunteer hours to the Red Cross.

"How do you find time for everything?" a newspaper reporter asked.

Myrtle smiled. "You don't find it; you make it!"

Armed with a camera, Myrtle scoured Hazelwood, taking pictures of nature's beautiful blooms and small animals. She enjoyed giving programs, especially in rest

homes where she could share those scenes that the residents might not be able to see for themselves.

After Myrtle had shown her slides of Hazelwood one evening, a frail old man came up to her.

"I remember Christmas roses like you showed," the man said, his eyes filled with tears. "My mother raised them on our farm. I never thought I'd see any again. You're a good lady to let us share your home like this."

Myrtle smiled, gently taking the man's hand. "Next time I come, I shall bring you a real Christmas rose," she promised.

The years slipped by quickly. Myrtle was forced to stay more at home, attending to her health.

In August of 1971, newspapers carried the reports of Myrtle Walgreen's death. She was ninety-one.

"Myrtle Walgreen filled many roles in her lifetime," wrote one newspaper editor. "Whether it be as a mother, a businesswoman, a wife, or public speaker, she proved herself capable and generous. Her life was unselfish— an example for people everywhere."

*   *   *

BIBLIOGRAPHY (Walgreen)

Walgreen, Myrtle. NEVER A DULL DAY. Chicago: Henry Regnery, 1963.

Obituary, New York: New York Times, August 22, 1971.

FRANCES WILLARD
1839-1898

Frances Willard, aged seven, sat between her father and her brother, Oliver, on the high seat of the covered wagon. It was a bumpy ride. Her sunbonnet was jostled loose and fell down around her shoulders showing her stubble-cut red hair.

"What did you ever cut your hair for, Frankie?" twelve year old Oliver grinned down at her.

Frances jumped down and ran up front to where Mama and Mary, Frances' five year old sister, were riding along in the buggy.

"He knows why I cut my hair," she murmured to herself as she jogged in rhythm with the sorrel gelding who was pulling the buggy. "I want people to think I'm a boy. Boys always get to do everything. Girls aren't supposed to do this or that or something else. Maybe with everybody calling me Frankie and with my hair short, I can do some of the things Oliver does."

"Frankie!" called her mother, "are you talking to yourself? Here, take the reins and watch your sister, Mary."

Frankie smiled at little blond Mary who was so pretty, so delicate, and so patient.

"We'll soon be in Chicago," she told Mary.

April's balmy weather turned to cold rain on the day before the travelers reached Chicago. Frankie wondered why they had made this journey.

Her father, Josiah Willard, was a hard working man. He was a dreamer and a scholar too. He must have inherited these traits from his distinguished ancestors, Samuel and Joseph Willard, both of whom had been Presidents of Harvard College. Frances' father was thrifty. He was a good businessman and made a large sum of money in his store in Churchville, New York. Frances was born in Churchville.

Frances was only two when the family moved from Churchville. At that time her father was looking for more cultural opportunities for himself and his family. He took them on a two hundred and eighty mile journey to Oberlin, Wisconsin.

At Oberlin he thought he could find time for the education he missed in his youth. He could study with the idea of entering the ministry. Besides, Oberlin College was coeducational and his wife, Mary, could enroll in some classes which were open to women.

Life at Oberlin was happy. Then disaster struck. Josiah Willard had a hemorrhage and the doctor said he must give up the classroom life and lead an outdoor life.

Frankie wondered why the family couldn't lead the outdoor life in Oberlin. But then her father thought a complete change would be best and the family usually did what Father told them to. Here they were, on their way to a cousin' of Mother's in Janesville, Wisconsin.

By the time the Willard party reached Chicago, its main streets were full of mud holes. Some of the holes had signs by them reading: "Bad hole. No Bottom!"

Mrs. Willard saw the discouraged look on her children's faces. She said: "Now children, don't forget, the name Willard means one who wills. Your family's motto is 'Patience rejoices in hardship.' "

On May 20, 1846, the weary Willards reached their goal. They drove up to Cousin Lemuel D. Thompson's home.

Frankie liked staying at Cousin Lemuel's farm with its spacious lawns. She played with the children, and Papa and the men traveled over the countryside looking at farms to buy.

Papa finally chose a farm. It was a fine stretch of fertile land on the banks of the Rock River. It was a perfect site with the river to the west, prairie to the east, low, wooded hills all around.

Papa named the farm Forest Home. Frankie thought it was a perfect name for the home so far from town.

Oliver was given a horse, Redbird. He and Redbird galloped over the open range and explored miles and miles of prairie. Frankie watched with envy.

One day Frankie asked her mother, "Why can't I own a horse? Why can't I ride too?"

"Because, dear," Mrs. Willard tried to explain, "your father says girls are expected to do household things after chores. He thinks girls should sew."

Frankie stamped her foot in exasipration.

Her father's health began improving immediately. He bought a hundred sheep, the Smithsonian Institute appointed him observer of the weather conditions in his district; he organized the Rock County Agricultural Association and served a term in the Wisconsin House of Representatives.

But Frankie could think only of Oliver going away. It would be lonely without him. Besides, Oliver was really needed on the farm. Still, Oliver presented such good arguments about going to college that he was allowed to go.

"Don't you get any such ideas as college, young lady," her father said. He hoisted Oliver's trunk into the wagon as he spoke.

Frankie felt resentment. She wanted to learn all there was in all the books she could put her hands on. And now her father was telling her that girls should not have those thoughts even while he was sending Oliver away to be educated. He had tolerated Mother's desire to learn rhetoric when they were in Oberlin.

Rebellion burned in Frankie's heart. She wanted a chance to learn.

Frankie did learn as the days went by. She and Mary learned botany and geology on the farm from their father. Mrs. Willard read them Addison, Cowper, and Tennyson.

Then Mr. Willard, with a small appropriation from the county, had a district school built for the neighborhood. It was the first real school Frances Willard went to and she loved it. She studied with ardor.

Mary studied hard too. Mary was almost a raving beauty by this time, or so Frances thought. Frankie admired the way Mary's hair hung in curls and her cheeks were pink like the dew-moistened roses.

"Well," Frankie told her mother one morning after church, "I'm homely, my hair is straight and red. My features aren't bad taken one by one, but all together they don't look like a doll's face like they do on

Mary.""Now, Frankie," Mrs. Willard protested, "to me you are beautiful!"

"Why couldn't Oliver be the homely one?" Frankie persisted. "He's handsome and has the right to do what he wants. It isn't fair!"

"Why, Frances Elizabeth Willard," her mother exclaimed, "what do you mean by that? We have always been fair with our children!"

"Oh," sighed Frankie, "it's not your fault. It's just the way things are. Boys get to go to college. They can swim, and ride horses whenever they want to . . . . . girls can't be as free as boys."

"You'll make your mark in the world just the same, Frankie," her mother consoled her. "With your ability to talk, people are sure to listen."

As the years slipped by, Frances and her father grew farther apart. Then, on her birthday, when she was eighteen, Frankie picked up a copy of IVANHOE.

Josiah Willard watched her as she drew the chair close to the fire and began scanning the pages of the book. He stood behind her and leaned closely in order to read what she was reading.

Frankie's heart pounded and her cheeks felt flushed. She waited for her father's infuriated comments.

His reaction was not long in coming, "Haven't I forbidden you to read novels?" her father shouted.

"Yes, Papa," Frankie answered him, "But I am eighteen today and considered no longer a child. I am a woman. A woman is entitled to express her own judgements and I am of the opinion that novels do not contaminate the mind of a woman anymore than they contaminate the mind of a man."

Frankie waited for her father's reaction. She was a bit surprised to see him smile a wry smile.

Frankie thought: "Papa has recognized his own fiery nature and devotion to justice in my statements."

Shortly after Frankie's eighteenth birthday Aunt Sarah Hill, her mother's sister, came to teach at the Milwaukee Female College. The two Willard girls were two of her first pupils. Mary was a fair student. Frankie went right to the top of the class. But after the holidays, Josiah Willard decided to take the girls out of school.

Frankie didn't know what made her father decide against school. She was furious about having to leave Milwaukee. She wrote in her diary that she had "never known the awareness of learning" as she had known it in Milwaukee. She seethed with resentment at being taken out of school. Mary accepted her father's decision without the slightest protest.

Her father now favored a college in Evanston, Illinois. The name of the Illinois school was Northwestern Female College. Frankie studied hard. She made a new friend, Kate Jackson. Kate was to be a great influence in her life.

Another unbelievable happening, after Frankie and Mary had been in Evanston for two years was that Josiah Willard liked Lake Michigan so much he sold Forest Home and the family moved again. He built a beautiful home in Evanston, facing the Lake. Oliver graduated from Beloit and he began his further studies at Garrett Bible Institute in Evanston. The family was all together again.

One day, a few weeks before Frankie was to graduate, the president of Northwestern Female College announced: "We have computed all the grade scores and we find the valedictorian to be . . . . ." he paused and Frankie's heart did a hiccup. Could she be the highest one in the class she wondered?

"The valedictorian is," Professor Jones went on smiling widely, "Miss Frances Willard."

Frankie bowed modestly as the girls clapped and clapped, but inside she was shouting wildly: "I did it. I got the highest honors at Northwestern just like Oliver did at Beloit!"

In the weeks that followed Frankie practiced her valedictorian speech so much that Mary pleaded with her to forget it for a while. Then, as graduation came closer, Frankie came down with a fever.

"Typhoid fever," the doctor said.

"Oh!" cried Frankie, "my greatest ambition has been blighted! All my composing and practicing is gone. I shall never be the same."

But she was very much the same after graduation. She was the same restless girl. She watched Mary at her drawing board and knew that such a quiet activity was not for her. Mary was getting frail and admitted that she felt too tired most of the time.

Finally, Frankie decided she would teach. Her father, reminding her constantly that he was well off financially, did not favor the idea.

Frankie said: "Teaching is one way I can help people, girls in particular. If girls are educated, they will be better able to raise their stations in life."

Her first school was a shabby school in a suburb of Chicago called Harlem. Most of the pupils were the children of German immigrants. Many teachers had failed here. But Frances established discipline and taught her pupils singing, Bible reading, and unheard of calisthenics. The children came to adore her. To show their affection they often brought her gifts of plants and kuchens.

That spring in Harlem, Oliver brought a friend of his

to visit. His name was Charles Fowler. He was a divinity student. Charles courted Frankie. They had long talks. Frankie's step was light and her laughter came easily.

"He told me he loves me," she confided to Mary.

By fall Frankie wasn't seeing Charles anymore. She broke the engagement without telling anyone why.

Frankie was saddened by her break with Charles, but she was more saddened by Mary's illness. One day Mary died.

It was hard for Frances to accept the fact that Mary was dead. Through grief, the restless search, the driving urge to serve, great stronger. She tried teaching a few classes at Northwestern Female College. Then she taught at Pittsburg Female College and wrote Mary's biography there.

Mr. Willard sold the Evanston home and built another smaller home in a similar location.

Then is 1866, the centennial of the Methodist Church in the United States was celebrated in Illinois by raising money for the Garrett Biblical Institute. Frances Willard was elected recording secretary, helped raise thirty thousand dollars, and was asked to write the dedicatory address for some man to read.

Then she accepted an invitation to teach at Genesee Welleyan Seminary in New York, met her old friend Kate Jackson, was entertained often in Kate's home, and made friends with Kate's father.

That Christmas Kate's father said: "I like you Frances Willard. In fact, I like you so much, I would like to include you in my daughter's Christmas present."

Frankie looked at him in astonishment.

Mr. Jackson, a wealthy manufacturer from Patterson, New Jersey, went on: "You two girls may go to Europe for a year or two, or as long as you like, with an unlimited spending account."

Frankie and Kate danced wildly about in unleashed joy. This was what Frankie had always wanted, the broadest of educations.

She and Kate did travel several years and became cultured ladies. They were popular wherever they went.

Frances Willard became Dean of Women at Northwestern University where she grew more and more interested in the progress of women.

The Association for the Advancement of Women was started with Frances Willard as Vice-President.

Then the end of the Civil War leashed upon the nation such drunkeness as the nation had never before experienced. In 1874 the Women's National Christian Temperance Union was organized with Frances as corresponding secretary. Five years later Frances Willard was the organization's president.

Her speeches were printed in newspapers here and abroad.

Frances Willard, the great leader of woman sufferage and of temperance, became one of America's most distinguished women and one of Illinois' most beloved women.

Frances Elizabeth Willard died in New York City February 17, 1898.

BIBLIOGRAPHY (Willard)

Alger, William R. FRIENDSHIPS OF WOMEN. Boston. Roberts Bros. 1890

Earhart, Mary. FRANCES WILLARD; FROM PRAYERS TO POLITICS. Chicago: University of Chicago Press, 1944

Shaw, Anna Howard. THE STORY OF A PIONEER. New York: Harper Bros. 1915

Trowbridge, Lydia Jones. FRANCES WILLARD OF EVANSTON. Chicago: Willett, Clark and Co., 1938

EPILOGUE

Illinois is fortunate to have had so many women "born to serve." The preceding twelve stories are only representative of thousands more that might have been included. Of the twelve stories, space limitations offer only a glimpse at the lives of these great women. Readers seeking further information may consult the bibliographical sources.

At different times and in different ways, the following women also provided unique and dedicated service. These "thumbnail sketches" may open the reader's door to further investigation of Illinois women "born to serve." Indeed, the list is endless. . .

MARY HUNTER AUSTIN
1869-1934

Mary Hunter was born in Carlinville, Illinois on September 9, 1868. Raised in a family torn by illness and frustration, Mary sought early fulfillment in writing happy fastasies.

Securing a teaching certificate, Mary gained personal freedom and independence. In May, 1891, she married Stafford Austin. Their lives in desert towns offered Mary much material for writing. She became highly respected for her work on Indian arts and culture.

Writing took her to many distant settings, each one offering background for a new book. She was in the midst of a new novel when she died August 13, 1934.

MYRA COLBY BRADWELL
1831-1894

Born February 12, 1831 in Vermont, Myra Colby later traveled west and received a teaching certificate from Elgin Seminary. After marrying Judge James Bradwell, she taught in the Chicago public schools.

In 1863 and 1865, Myra Bradwell served as president of the Soldiers' Aid Society and was the leading spirit in the Sanitary Fairs held in Chicago.

After the Civil War, Myra began the study of law. In 1868 she started the publication "The Chicago Legal News."

After passing a creditable exam, Myra applied for admission to the bar in 1871. She was denied on the sole ground of sex by both the Illinois and United States Supreme Courts.

Undaunted, Myra continued her fight for bar admission. It was finally granted in 1892, Thus she became the first Illinois woman lawyer. She died two years later.

JEAN BROWNING
(1918-1972)

"She had the voice of an angel."

So wrote a New York Times music critic on the death of Jean Browning in 1972. Only fifty-four at the time of her death, she had brought joy to millions through music.

Born in Centralia in 1918, Jean showed a musical interest early in life. Gifted both in voice and piano, she directed her major attention to voice while studying at Juilliard School of Music. She also met her husband, Francis Madeira at Juilliard, and they were married in 1947.

Receiving only minor roles at the Metropolitan Opera in New York, Jean traveled to Italy where she experienced immediate success. She made her debut in "Carmen" and received forty-five curtain calls! Returning to the United States, she enjoyed a fifteen year reign as a star of the Metropolitan Opera from 1956 to 1971. Her voice could span three octaves with depth and feeling. Her death saddened opera lovers around the world.

KATHERINE DEERE BUTTERWORTH
1866-1953

Katherine Mary Deere was born October 13, 1866 in Moline, Illinois. She was grandaughter of the developer of the first steel plow, John Deere.

With her marriage to lawyer William Butterworth, Katherine became an active force behind numerous community service causes. Both Mr. and Mrs. Butterworth campaigned and worked actively for the American Red Cross and the Visiting Nurses Association.

Katherine Butterworth continued her community involvement after her husband's death in 1936. Following her own death in 1953, her will revealed that the Butterworth family home would be used as a community center for arts, health and civic organizations. Soon afterwards, a grade school in Moline was named Butterworth after the woman who wished to be remembered as a "good citizen with a willing heart."

ISABELLA LANING CANDEE
(1850-1931)

Isabella Laning was a girl of nine when her family moved from Pennsylvania to LaSalle in 1859. She received her education at Monticello and Rockford Seminaries. After a brief teaching career, she married Henry Hinsdale Candee in 1868 and moved to Cairo.

In Cairo, Isabella took a keen interest in community affairs. She helped start the Cairo Women's Club and the Library Association. Her dedicated efforts began capturing statewide attention.

In 1894, Isabella became the first president of the Illinois Federation of Women's Clubs. Displaying a compassionate regard for the poor, she led programs that helped assist the unemployed and distressed during the bad economic times of the late 1890's.

She died in Chicago in 1931.

MARY HARTWELL CATHERWOOD
1844-1902

Mary Hartwell contributed poems to local newspapers when she was a small girl.

As she grew older she believed her talent for writing was in prose and not in poetry. The first prose for which she was paid was "The Mill-Scott Million."

Later in her life she enjoyed writing subjects connected with Illinois history. She published popular novels with Illinois backgrounds. Two of the titles were "The Story of Tonty" and "Old Kaskaskia".

Married to James S. Catherwood, the couple made their home in Hoopeston, Illinois. Mary Hartwell Catherwood died December 26, 1902.

138

RACHEL CROTHERS
1878-1958

"With the enlightening and sparkling play, 'A Little Journey,' the professional status of playright Rachel Crothers is most secure."

That item in "Variety" was only one reward to be given Rachel Crothers in 1918. Her play, "A Little Journey," was also nominated for a Pulitzer Prize in Drama.

Born December 12, 1878, in Bloomington, Illinois, Rachel soon became interested in the theatre. She studied theatre on the east coast, becoming an instructor. Gradually her interest turned to writing, a career which produced a number of Broadway hits.

At the age of eighty, Rachel Crothers died July 5, 1958.

VIRGINIA SNIDER EIFERT
1911-1966

Born in 1911, Virginia Snider received her schooling in Springfield, Illinois. She married Herman Eifert in 1936.

Always a nature enthusiast, in 1939 Virginia became editor of "Living Museum," a small magazine published by the Illinois State Museum. Due largely to Virginia's fascinating articles and illustrations, the magazine's readership skyrocketed—from 1,000 to 25,000. In addition to her contributions to "Living Museum," Virginia brought new spotlight to Abe Lincoln, the Delta Queen riverboat, the Mississippi River—all via her books.

Readers everywhere mourned the news of her passing on June 17, 1966.

HELEN SCOTT HAY
(1869-1932)

While Civil War nurse Clara Barton was working to establish an American nursing service in 1869, Helen Scott Hay was born in Lanark, Illinois. In time, Barton's national Red Cross would play a vital part in Helen's life.

Graduating from Savannah High School in 1886, Helen pursued education further as both a teacher and a student. Discovering a major interest in medical services, she turned to nursing.

After serving as head nurse in Iowa and California hospitals, Helen became actively involved with Red Cross activities. In 1914, she led a "Mercy Mission" to Europe. During World War I, she served as Director of Home Hygiene and Care of the Sick. She was officially commended by President Woodrow Wilson for her service. Later she served as Director of American Nursing in Europe.

Returning to Savannah to care for her brother, John, during his final illness, Helen Scott Hay died November 25, 1932.

SARAH MARSHALL HAYDEN
1825-1899

Sarah Marshall was born in Shawneetown, Illinois.

At the age of sixteen, Sarah Marshall wrote a novel which was published thirteen years later. The novel received great praise.

Mrs. Hayden was the first woman novelist of Illinois. "Early Engagements" and its sequel, "Florence," were published in 1854. For almost sixty years Mrs. Hayden wrote for magazines and newspapers, poetry as well as prose.

HELEN ELNA HOKINSON
1893-1949

Helen Elna Hokinson was born in Mendota, Illinois. She became well known for her cartoons, which often appeared in leading magazines.

She studied at the Chicago Academy of Fine Arts and then began a career in commercial design and fashion. Her caricatures won her lasting fame, as well as many laughs along the way.

ANNA WILMARTH ICKES
1873-1935

A tragic auto accident in New Mexico on August 31, 1935 removed an exciting, dynamic woman from the national scene. Across the country, people mourned the death of Anna Ickes.

Born and raised in Chicago, Anna Wilmarth enjoyed a childhood of wealth and comfort. Her father was a manufacturer of gas fixtures, while Anna's mother was a leader of women's reform movements.

Anna developed an early interest in politics. In 1911, she married Harold Ickes, a lawyer who shared her political interests. With Harold as her campaign manager, Anna won election to the Illinois State Legislature three times. Her travels west also offered her a chance to share publicly her concerns with the Indians of America.

FLORENCE KELLEY
(1859-1942)

"It is never too late to change," Florence Kelley said often. Clearly she took her own advice.

Born in Philadelphia in 1859, Florence was ill much of her childhood. Only a determined spirit helped her graduate from Cornell University with a Social Studies degree. She traveled to Europe, married a doctor and began raising a family. After the marriage failed, she brought her children back and joined Jane Addams at Hull House.

At the time, working children had few laws protecting them. Florence directed her efforts establishing programs to make factories provide care and safety for youthful workers. She was named Commissioner of the Illinois Factory Inspection Department when it was created.

Her death, in 1942, at the age of eighty-three, removed a champion of children's rights from the American scene.

MADAME LA COMPT
1734-1843

Miss LaFlamme married and lived in Chicago in 1765. After her husband, Sainte Ange, died she married a Canadian whose name was M.La Compt. From this marriage came one of the largest French families in Illinois.

The Indians were her friends and neighbors all her life. By a wise and good relationship with them she acquired a great influence over the Pottawatomies, Kickapoos, and other Indians who bordered the Great Lakes, and in this way was able to prevent many an Indian attack on the white population.

JULIA CLIFFORD LATHROP
(1858-1932)

Born in Rockford in 1858, Julia Clifford Lathrop attended area schools and graduated from Vassar College in Poughkeepsie, New York. After serving as her father's secretary, Julia went to work at Hull House.

An expert at compiling reports, Julia devoted herself to putting together records about the tragic conditions of insane asylums and poorhouses.

But her main interest was youth. She dedicated her time and talents to assist juvenile delinquents and illegitimate children. Both Presidents Taft and Wilson appointed her to national commissions. Her ten years of service provided many new programs, including the establishment of juvenile courts.

In 1932, Julia died in Rockford.

JEAN KENYON MACKENZIE
1874-1936

Born January 6, 1874 in Elgin, Jean MacKenzie was the eldest of six children. Her father was minister and college professor.

Following her studies at Van Ness Seminary in San Francisco, the Sorbonne in Paris and the University of California, Jean volunteered as a missionary to Africa. For ten years she worked among the "bush natives" until an accident forced her return to America. Thus began an extensive writing and speaking career, an effort that brought Americans an awareness and understanding of the African people. She died September 2, 1936, a victim of lung cancer.

EDITH ROCKEFELLER MCCORMICK
1872-1932

Edith McCormick founded the Chicago Zoological Gardens.

"We must get closer to animals," she declared, "to reach the human soul."

Edith Rockefeller McCormick maintained during her life, the proud reserve and dignity which characterized her earlier prominence in Chicago society.

"Edith Rockefeller McCormick established guidelines for good manners and grace," wrote one newspaper editor upon her death in 1932.

MARIE JOSEEPHA MERGLER
1851-1901

Marie Mergler was born May 18, 1851, in Bavaria. Her father was a physician who brought his family to Palatine, Illinois, when Marie was only two.

Marie's schooling led her into teaching, but she felt dissatisfied and unfulfilled. Further study brought her a degree in medicine, where she found acceptance and admiration as an administrator of hospitals and schools. Recognized as a gifted surgeon, she died in 1901, the day before her fiftieth birthday.

LOTTIE HOLMAN O'NEILL
(1878-1967)

Lottie Holman O'Neill was first elected to the Illinois legislature as a representative from DuPage County in 1922.

Her most famous bill introduced the eight hour day for women in Illinois. Another increased state aid for the care and education of handicapped children.

Lottie Holman O'Neill will be remembered for the distinction of having held a state office longer than any other woman in the country, having served in the senate as well as the legislature, and for being the first woman to enter Illinois politics.

ALICE FREEMAN PALMER
1855-1902

Alice Palmer was President of Wellesley College for six years and Dean of Women at the University of Chicago for three.

She often "took to the platform" in behalf of girls' colleges. Her audiences were swayed by her good looks and delightful personality and became advocates of higher education for women.

"I am trying to make girls wiser and happier," she is quoted as saying.

Her many students testified to her accomplishments. "She opened a whole new world of poetry and music and lovely ideas," one of her students said. "We always called her ' "the beautiful lady.' "

HARRIET SANGER PULLMAN
1842-1921

Harriet Sanger was born in Chicago. In 1867 she married George M. Pullman.

The Pullman home was the center of social activity over which she presided with grace and dignity.

Mrs. Pullman served on the board of the old Mary Thompson Hospital for Women and Children, left a substantial legacy to St. Luke's Hospital, supported the Pullman Public Library, and gave much time and money during the years of World War I for relief work.

She helped many musical students to study abroad.

Her sympathy was always with the poor and she gave generously to help them.

MARY JANE SAFFORD
1834-1891

Born December 31, 1834, Mary Jane was only three when her family moved from Vermont to a farm near Crete, Illinois. After obtaining teaching qualifications, she taught in the Cairo area.

The outbreak of the Civil War in 1861 caused Mary Jane to change roles—from teacher to nurse. Working closely with "Mother" Bickerdyke, she filled whatever position was needed. After the war, she obtained an M. D. Degree. Her medical practice in Chicago flourished until failing health forced her retirement in 1886. She died five years later.

FRANCES WOOD SHIMER
1826-1901

In childhood Frances Ann Wood loved books. And because she was so widely read, she began teaching at the age of fifteen. She decided to get more formal education.

After she graduated from Normal School in Albany, New York, she heard of an opportunity for opening a new school at Mt. Carroll, Illinois. She and a classmate decided to undertake the school. In 1853 they opened a school for boys and girls.

She was an educator with broad vision as well as a woman of sensitivity and dedication.

SARAH HACKETT STEVENSON
(1841-1909)

John Hackett Stevenson was a pioneer, in fact, he opened the first store in Buffalo Grove, Illinois. It was in this small town that Sarah Ann Hackett Stevenson was born in 1841.

An intense interest in science brought Sarah to Chicago where she immersed herself in studying medicine. After obtaining her degree in 1875, she began practicing her profession. Soon she became a pioneer herself, becoming the first female member of the American Medical Association, first woman appointed to the Cook County Hospital staff and the first woman appointed to the Illinois State Board of Health.

Sarah fought for better medical education for females and many humanitarian programs. She died in 1909 at the age of sixty-eight.

MARION TALBOT
(1858-1948)

The American Association of University Women is one of the most active organizations in the country. To its founder, Marion Talbot, much credit should be given.

A distinguished student, she gained both a Bachelor and Master's Degree from Boston University.

Using an idea formulated by her mother, Marion founded the Association of College Alumnae which later became the AAUW. Her co-workers were Ellen Richards and Alice Freeman.

Marion became Dean of Undergraduate Women at the University of Chicago in 1892. Home Economics was a special interest, and she wrote many books on the subject. Queen Victoria of England called Marion, "Illinois' most outstanding citizen."

Marion Talbot died in 1948, but the AAUW is an active, ongoing memorial to her energy.

CATHARINE VAN VALKENBURG WAITE
1829-1913

Born January 30, 1829 in Canada, Catharine Van Valkenburg was 21 before she arrived in Illinois to study at Knox College in Galesburg. In 1854, she married a Chicago lawyer named Charles Waite. Spurred by his legal activities, Catharine became active in women's suffrage. In 1869 she and her husband helped found the Illinois Woman Suffrage Association.

Catharine's activities in behalf of women's rights were interrupted six times—to have children. Granted a law degree in 1886, Catharine chose to share her legal expertise through writing in newspapers and law journals. She died November 9, 1913.

MAY THIELGAARD WATTS
(1893-1975)

Illinois nature lovers surely had a champion in May Thielgaard Watts. Since her birth in 1893, she carried a love for nature all her life.

Graduating from the University of Chicago in 1918 with a degree in botany, May taught school in Wilmette.

May raised an interest among Illinoisans in nature. Through speeches and writings, she sought a place where people could walk and enjoy the feel of the prairie. Her prime target was the old Chicago, Aurora and Elgin Railroad right-of-way. In 1965, this area was labeled the "Illinois Prairie Path," with most of it designated as part of the National Trails System.

By her writing, speaking and founding of the Illinois Prairie Path, May had brought a new appreciation of nature to countless people before she died in 1975.

MARY ALLEN WEST
1837-1893

Mary Allen West, educator and philanthropist, was born at Galesburg, Illinois.

In 1873 she was elected County Superintendent of Schools, serving nine years.

Mary Ellen West always took an interest in educational and reformatory movements.

For several years she was editor of "Our Home Monthly" and was Editor-in-Chief of "The Union Signal," the magazine of the Women's Christian Temperance Union of which she became president.

She will also be remembered as president of the Illinois Woman's Press Association of Chicago.

ABOUT THE AUTHORS . . .

David R. Collins

David R. Collins received his BS and MS Degrees from Western Illinois University. With advanced study at Indiana University, the University of Wisconsin and the University of Colorado, Collins is presently an English instructor at Woodrow Wilson Junior High School in Moline, Illinois.

Founder of the Mississippi Valley Writers Conference and the Children's Literature Festival, Collins has won national writing recognition from the Junior Literary Guild, UNESCO and the Freedom Foundation at Valley Forge, Pennsylvania. Among his other books are LINDA RICHARDS, FIRST AMERICAN TRAINED NURSE; FOOTBALL RUNNING BACKS; HARRY S. TRUMAN, PEOPLE'S PRESIDENT; CHARLES LINDBERGH, HERO PILOT; IF I COULD, I WOULD (all published by Garrard Publishing Company); ABRAHAM LINCOLN; GEORGE WASHINGTON CARVER; FRANCIS SCOTT KEY (published by Mott Media); THE ONE BAD THING ABOUT BIRTHDAYS (Harcourt Brace); DOROTHY DAY; GEORGE MEANY; THOMAS MERTON (St. Anthony Messenger Press) and the JOSHUA POOLE series published by Broadman Press.

Evelyn Witter

Evelyn Witter, a Chicago native, presently resides in Milan, Illinois. A graduate of the University of Illinois, she has taken advanced study at Northwestern University, Indiana University and the University of Colorado.

A creative writing instructor with Black Hawk College, Witter is the author of thousands of magazine stories and articles. Her Jenny Marsh mystery series, published by Children's Press, includes THE MYSTERY OF THE RED BRICK HOUSE; THE MYSTERY OF ANIMAL HAVEN; THE MYSTERY OF THE ROLLTOP DESK; THE MYSTERY OF THE MISSING BICYCLES; THE MYSTERY OF MUSIC IN THE NIGHT and THE MYSTERY OF THE RED-EYED CAMEL PIN. Her biography of ABIGAIL ADAMS in the Mott Media Sowers Series has proven a best seller, while IN JESUS' DAY is a popular offering from Concordia Publishing Company. THE LOCKED DRAWER was recently published by Broadman Press. Another volume, FUN AROUND THE WORLD, is forthcoming from Broadman, while additional titles of Jenny Marsh mysteries are scheduled for Children's Press.

If you wish to order additional copies of Notable Illinois Women, please send $6.95 plus 85¢ tax and handling to:
Quest Publishing
2018-29th Street
Rock Illinois, Illinois
61201